# A
# Not-So-Silent
# Night

# A
# Not-So-Silent
# Night

· · · · · · · · · · · ·

**THE UNHEARD STORY OF CHRISTMAS
AND WHY IT MATTERS**

· · · · · · · · · · · ·

## VERLYN D. VERBRUGGE

*A Not-So-Silent Night: The Unheard Story of Christmas and Why It Matters*

© 2009 by Verlyn D. Verbrugge

Published by Kregel Publications, a division of Kregel, Inc., P.O. Box 2607, Grand Rapids, MI 49501.

**Library of Congress Cataloging-in-Publication Data**
    Verbrugge, Verlyn D.
    A not-so-silent night : the unheard story of Christmas and why it matters / Verlyn D. Verbrugge.
       p.   cm.
    Includes bibliographical references.
    1. Christmas.  I. Title.
    BV45.V46        2009        232.92—dc22        2009019034

ISBN 978-0-8254-3909-4

Printed in the United States of America

09  10  11  12  13 / 5  4  3  2  1

*To Lori*
*The love of my life*

# Contents

# Acknowledgments

I had been thinking about writing this book for many years. Two things happened in 2008 that made it clear to me that this was the year I was supposed to do so. In the summer of 2008, my family was preparing to go to Trinidad, where I was going to teach a one-week class in 1 Corinthians, but those plans suddenly fell through. And that fall I was going to teach a course in some of Paul's letters at a local Christian college, but that opportunity fell through as well. So with extra time on my hands, I felt the Lord was telling me, "I have orchestrated these things to give you the time to put down in writing your thoughts about the dark side of Christmas."

I am indeed grateful to the Lord for the privilege I have had to spend my life studying and learning about his holy Word—as a seminary student, as a full-time pastor, and as an academic editor at one of the major evangelical Christian publishing companies. Moreover, I am indebted to him for giving me a good mind to delve into the riches of the Scriptures.

I'm appreciative, too, for the many people who have heard me talk about the themes of this book. I began preaching about the dark side of Christmas when I was pastor at the Southern Heights Christian Reformed Church in Kalamazoo, Michigan, and I have continued such messages with those who attend the weekly services I lead at the Woodland Drive-In Church in Grand Rapids. Their appreciation for this theme of Christmas has meant much to me. And I thank the many others with whom I have shared these ideas and who have become enthusiastic to hear more. Their reception has encouraged me to write this book.

I am thankful, too, to Kregel Publications for their willingness to publish this book. I thank Jack Kragt for putting me in touch with editor Jim Weaver and for being a cheerleader for this book. I'm grateful as well for Jim's enthusiasm for my manuscript and for shepherding this book through the editorial process. To the other employees at Kregel who have worked on different phases of this book, I thank you from the bottom of my heart.

Finally, I want to thank my wife, Lori, to whom this book is dedicated, for her support while this book was being written. She read through the entire manuscript and offered many fine suggestions on how to improve it. For that I am deeply appreciative.

# Introduction

A lot of cultural mythology is associated with how we perceive Christmas and with how we celebrate the traditions of the Christmas season:

- It's a time for joy and happiness and the singing of cheery Christmas carols.
- It's a time for family get-togethers and feasting on all sorts of special goodies.
- It's a time for the giving and receiving of gifts. And who doesn't like to get gifts? Giving has, in fact, become so central to Christmas, we even have expressions connected with that part of our tradition. A poor family whose children do not receive gifts because they can't afford them and don't receive them through some community program "don't have a Christmas." As another expression—a local chain store advertises that because their prices are lower, you can "buy so much more Christmas."

- It's a time for brightly colored lights and decorated trees.
- It's a time for special church services with Advent candles and sometimes even a live nativity scene.
- Above all, it's a time for peace—peace that we define primarily as the absence of conflict.

For a brief time each year we get to forget about the world of war and battle; the world of Iraq, Afghanistan, and the Middle East; the world of al-Qaida and the threat of global terrorism. I suspect that almost every preacher has told the story of Christmas 1914 on the western front of World War I, which has reached legendary status.[1] The opposing German and British soldiers spontaneously called a cease-fire and spent the day fraternizing in no-man's-land between their two military lines, singing Christmas carols, and even playing a soccer match (which reportedly ended when the soccer ball hit a barbed wire fence and deflated). The following day they were once again attempting to kill each other with machine guns. Subsequent wars have also seen declarations of a temporary cease-fire on Christmas Day. It just seems right for that day.

Is this not as it should be? Isn't Christmas the one day of the year when we should least think about military issues and battle-field imagery? And isn't it the time for "peace on earth," if only symbolically?

In all our Christmas traditions we think we're correctly reflecting the teachings of the Bible on the first Christmas. After all, Christmas is about a young woman visited by an angel to tell her that she would be the mother of the Messiah, the Son of David. The story continues with the birth of a cute, cuddly baby, Jesus, lying in a manger in soft, sweet hay and surrounded by lowing cattle. Then there's that choir of angels singing the first joyous Christmas carol to some shepherds on the fields of Bethlehem: "Glory to God in the highest, and on earth peace, good will toward men" (Luke 2:14 KJV). And this was followed by three wise kings from the Orient, who came to the manger with camels laden with presents for that baby in order to celebrate his joyous birth.

If that's what we read in the Scriptures, we have a lot to learn. Matthew 1 and 2 and Luke 1 and 2, read in the context of the rest of the Scriptures and in light of the culture of that day, tell a different story. The difference between that first Christmas and our contemporary view of Christmas as reflected in our celebrations is, in fact, the difference between day and night, between light and darkness.

There is a dark side to Christmas in the Bible, though we usually choose to ignore it. There is a profound sadness that permeates the various episodes in the Christmas story, and it's important for us to see that sadness. Furthermore, Christmas, rather than being the beginning of the age of peace, was in reality the beginning of war.

This book is about that dark side of Christmas. I don't deny that the end result of the Christmas story, seen in the light of the cross and resurrection, is the triumph of victory and life and light and peace. But for the characters in the Christmas story itself, especially Joseph and Mary, an aura of profound heaviness pervades the above-mentioned four chapters of the Bible. I maintain that until we see the dark side of Christmas, until we shed tears with Mary and Joseph, until we experience the fear held by the principal players in the Christmas story that war was on the horizon, we will never truly understand the awesomeness of what happened in that little town of Bethlehem.

Perhaps we can compare Christmas to the story of Good Friday. Why do we call the Friday of the crucifixion, which we observe each spring, *Good* Friday? Why do we call that day a day of hope? Why do we think of light when that day in history encompassed three hours of pitch-black darkness? For our Savior himself, Good Friday was anything but good. It was a day of incredible pain and suffering. It was the hour "when darkness reigns" (Luke 22:53). The only reason we call it *Good* Friday is because it was good *for us*, not because it was good for our Lord Jesus Christ.

So, too, with Christmas. While we can now look back at that day with hope and joy and peace, for the main characters within those familiar stories it was a time of sorrow and pain and rejection and danger. A careful reading of the Scriptures in the context of what we know about the politics and culture of the day will confirm that for us.

Let me share with you a story. One of my first opportunities when I began working as an editor at Zondervan was to write some of the devotions for what eventually was called *The Daylight Devotional Bible*. This was a Bible that had 365 devotions scattered throughout the entire Bible. My task was mostly to write devotions for special days and seasons, such as Advent, Valentine's Day, Lent, Good Friday, Easter, Mother's Day, Memorial Day, Thanksgiving Day, and the like. In one of my devotions for Advent, I wrote something about the heaviness and darkness that pervades the traditional Christmas stories in the New Testament. The person who was editing my devotions came to me and said, "We can't put that in our Bible. That's not what people are looking for at Christmastime. Christmas is a time for joy and peace and love." And so I rewrote the devotion.

That book, perhaps, was not the best occasion to make a point. But now it is time to pay close attention, not to our Christmas mythology, but to the Christmas stories in the Bible. There is such sadness in these episodes. But through our tears and our fears as we reflect on these stories, I pray that we may begin to hear what the Bible really tells us about the first Christmas. Let's begin our examination of this not-so-silent night.

## CHAPTER 1

# Born to Die

The birth of a baby is an exciting event, or at least it should be. Many, if not most, mothers-to-be are delighted at the prospect of giving birth. They may have apprehensions about the labor and delivery, but for the most part they are eagerly looking forward to the big day. Those who want to become pregnant but are unable to often carry a heavy burden in their hearts.

Naturally, during the time of pregnancy, the mother's heart is filled with many concerns and questions. Will the pregnancy go smoothly? Will any problems develop as the child grows and comes to full term? How will the labor and delivery proceed? Will the baby be normal? Will there be any birth defects—either defects that are already developing in the womb or that come as a result of a difficult delivery?

To a large extent, some of these questions can be, at least partially, answered today. With the development of ultrasound technology, a living child can be detected in the womb as early as four or five weeks. As the fetus develops, its features can be determined: five fingers on each hand, five toes on each foot. By the end of the fourth month, in many cases, the sex of the child can be determined. Doctors can assure the mother-to-be through an ultrasound that "everything is normal." It is even possible to do surgery on a child while it is still in the mother's womb.

This modern technology, though, can bring its own list of concerns. Before my youngest daughter was born, the doctor examined the data from one of my wife's ultrasounds and determined that there was something unusual about the umbilical cord. It had one artery leading from the placenta to the baby and one vein returning back to the placenta; most umbilical cords have two veins returning. Sometimes that phenomenon can be an indicator of birth defects. We would not have known that possibility without the ultrasound. As it turned out, baby Sarah was fine, for which we are thankful.

All of this is to say that we hope and we expect babies to be born alive and healthy. That is, after all, the way God intended it. Babies are born to live healthy and productive lives. It's always an exciting moment when a newborn takes his or her first breath. This life comes as a gift from God. If a mother-to-be experiences a miscarriage or a stillborn child, a deep cloud comes over her heart. It is equally traumatic when a baby is born with a life-threatening defect. In one of the churches I served, a baby was born with a weakened heart and, before he was three weeks old, had three open-heart surgeries. The child died at about four weeks, and it was truly a sad moment for the entire congregation. So many prayers—but the child died.

Babies are born to live—their first breath and every future breath coming as a gift from God. The apostle Paul affirmed this in his message to the meeting of the Areopagus, that God "gives everyone life and breath and everything else" (Acts 17:25). Or as Isaiah proclaimed so many years ago, the Lord, who "spread out the earth with all that springs from it . . . gives breath to its people, and life to those who walk on it" (Isa. 42:5). Babies are born to live, not die.

All babies—except one! That baby is the baby in the Christmas story. The whole New Testament, in fact, breathes the message that Jesus Christ, the babe of Bethlehem, *was born in order to die!*

In Galatians 4:4, Paul writes that when God's set time had fully come, God sent his Son in order to redeem us so that we might be adopted as his sons and daughters. That was the purpose of his coming into the world, and the price of that redemption was "the precious blood of Christ, a lamb without blemish or defect" (1 Peter 1:19). God sent his Son into the world and "presented Christ as a sacrifice of atonement, through the shedding of his blood" (Rom. 3:25). Based on the Old Testament analogy, a sacrifice of atonement meant, by its very nature, the death of the one whose blood was shed. In Old Testament Israel, every firstborn male animal belonged to the Lord and was to be sacrificed to him (Exod. 13:12; Num. 18:17).[1]

The writer of the letter to the Hebrews testifies that when Christ came into this world, he "came as high priest of the good things that are now already here" (Heb. 9:11). When a high priest in the Old Testament entered the Most Holy Place in the tabernacle or temple, he had to enter with blood from a sacrifice. Jesus entered the true Holy Place, heaven, not with the blood of some slain animal; rather, he "entered the Most Holy Place once for all by his own blood, thus obtaining eternal redemption" (v. 12). Jesus came into this world not only as God's heaven-sent high priest, but also as the Lamb that was slain, with whose blood he "purchased for God members of every tribe and language and people and nation" (Rev. 5:9). That was the purpose for his entrance into the world.

It is not, of course, that Jesus came into this world unwillingly.

When James and John, the sons of Zebedee, came to Jesus to ask to sit on his right and left hands, Jesus ended that discussion with a clear statement of why he voluntarily came into the world, not "to be served, but to serve, and to give his life as a ransom for many" (Mark 10:45). To give his life! Again, Jesus was born in order to die. Or—in the language once again of the writer to the Hebrews, who presents Jesus as using the words of Psalm 40—he "came into the world . . . 'to do your will, my God'" (Heb. 10:5–7).

Jesus himself said the same thing in the gospel of John, "For I have come down from heaven not to do my will but to do the will of him who sent me" (John 6:38). As Jesus continued his conversation with the Jews in John 6 as to the purpose of his coming into the world, he made it plain that he had come down from heaven to be the bread of life, which is his flesh, "which I will give for the life of the world" (v. 51). In other words, the will of the Father, which Jesus voluntarily followed, was for him to be "obedient to death— even death on a cross" (Phil. 2:8). Yet again, Jesus was born to die.

One aspect of the story of the visit of the magi recorded in Matthew 2 confirms that death was in the air at the time of their visit to Bethlehem. When they entered the house where Jesus was staying with his parents, they "presented him with gifts of gold, frankincense and myrrh" (v. 11). Myrrh is a spice from a tree found in Arabia, having cosmetic value and medicinal value as a pain reliever (see Mark 15:23). But myrrh was also used for embalming the body of a dead person, most notably, Jesus himself (see John 19:39). It is significant, perhaps, that the two uses of the noun *smyrna* ("myrrh") and the one use of the related verb *smyrnizo* ("to mix with myrrh") in the New Testament occur in the scenes of the birth of Jesus and the death of Jesus. From the time of his birth, death was already in the air.

During special Christian holidays such as Christmas and Easter, I often looked forward to Johnny Hart's *B.C.* comic strip. The late writer of this comic strip often wove a subtle—and sometimes not so subtle—Christian theme into his Sunday editions. One year, as I recall, the strip consisted of a drawing of the nativity scene with a large shadow cast over the area. As the frames of the comic strip progressed, it became clear that the shadow had the shape of a cross. We don't usually see that shadow in our celebrations of Christmas.

But it should be there. That's a biblical message. Already from the time of his birth, the shadow of a cross was cast over the manger. Yes, Jesus, the babe of Bethlehem, was the omnipotent Son of God, the second person of the Trinity, born as a mortal human being. In this he was unique. But he was also unique in another way. Human beings are born to live, including those who do not survive, making their death so shortly after birth incredibly tragic. In contrast, the Christmas child was born to die—born to give his life for the world.

## CHAPTER 2

# The Beginning
# of War

War is a terrifying event. With our television sets and reporters on the spot, we can see in our living rooms the fear and terror that war brings to unarmed civilians—children, women, and the elderly. Hundreds of thousands of people become refugees, fleeing for their lives to a place they hope is safe, leaving everything else behind. I've never been in or fought in a war, but I know people who have. They tell me that war is as close to hell on earth as one can get.

You may be surprised to hear this, but when you look closely at the stories in the Bible about the birth of Jesus, you can't help but realize that the first Christmas was the beginning of war. No, it was not the beginning of a war fought in the human world, though it did have an impact at least on some human beings. It was primarily the beginning of war in the celestial realm. But it was war nonetheless, and war is terrifying.

In the previous chapter, we saw that Jesus was born in order to die. His dying was not, however, the only reason stated in the Scriptures for why the Son of God came into this world. The apostle John puts it differently in 1 John 3:8: "The reason the Son of God appeared was to destroy the devil's work." That is, Jesus came into this world to destroy the frightening work that the Devil, working through the serpent in Genesis 3, had instigated at the dawn of history. The serpent succeeded in tempting Adam and Eve to sin against God. As a result, sin came into the world, and death came as a result of sin: "for dust you are and to dust you will return" (Gen. 3:19). God himself had said prior to that fateful event, the eating of the fruit of the forbidden tree, "You are free to eat from any tree in the garden; but you must not eat from the tree of the knowledge of good and evil, for when you eat of it you will certainly die" (Gen. 2:16–17).

Consequently, even though we are born to live, the reality is that we will all die because we all have sinned. "Therefore, just as sin entered the world through one man, and death through sin . . . in this way death came to all people, because all sinned" (Rom. 5:12). The Devil had managed to undo the promise of God to Adam and Eve that they could live forever. The task, therefore, that God had given to his Son, Jesus, was to share our humanity "so that by his death he might break the power of him who holds the power of death—that is, the devil" (Heb. 2:14). Jesus' goal, then, was to break the power of the Devil and to destroy his evil work.

But the Devil was not going to take that goal of Jesus lying down. He had no intention of quietly giving up and succumbing to the power of Christ. He was not going to simply yield to the power of God in Christ and fade away. Satan was equally intent on destroying Jesus. The moment Jesus was born, the Devil set in motion an orchestrated plan to destroy Jesus. Christmas was thus the beginning of war—war between the Son of God and the Devil.

The first skirmish began in the Christmas story—in that part of the story we don't read very often during the month of December. In the story of the magi's coming to Bethlehem, we stop our reading with the magi in the house, kneeling down to worship Jesus and presenting to him their gifts of gold, frankincense, and myrrh. Or perhaps we carry the story one verse further, where the magi leave Bethlehem by another way because they had been warned in a dream not to return to Herod.

But that is not the end of the story. Satan knew that he had been outsmarted by God. The Devil's intent had been to have the magi return to Jerusalem to tell Herod precisely where the new-born "king of the Jews" could be found. With that information Herod would, he had promised, go to worship the child as the magi had done (Matt. 2:8). His hidden purpose, however, was to order his soldiers to find the Christ child and murder him.

After the magi had left for home by a different route, Satan had to move to plan 2; he inspired the wicked King Herod, who would tolerate no rivals, to order his soldiers "to kill all the boys in Bethlehem and its vicinity who were two years old and under, in accordance with the time he had learned from the Magi" (Matt. 2:16). By destroying all the infants and toddler boys in Bethlehem and its environs, Herod could be sure that the new rival king would also be killed. Only by a miraculous intervention was Jesus spared the sword of Herod, for the angel of the Lord appeared to Joseph in a dream and warned him to flee to Egypt immediately with Mary and the baby (Matt. 2:13).

This was only the end of one battle, however, not the end of the war. The war continued. We have no idea how many attempts on the life of Jesus the Devil may have instigated during Jesus' boy-hood and early manhood. But we do know that there were at least six more attempts on Jesus' life during the years of his ministry.

The first attempt comes in the temptation of Jesus by the Devil in the desert. There, Satan tries to goad Jesus to jump down from the pinnacle of the temple in order to display to the people his awesome power. Satan even quotes Psalm 91:11–12, assuring Jesus that he will receive protection from God's angels (Matt. 4:5–7; Luke 4:9–12). But Jesus refuses to jump in a suicidal death leap, knowing that he would be disobeying God and that God does not rescue those who deliberately tempt him.

The next incident occurs when Jesus is in Nazareth, preaching in the synagogue to the people he grew up with. He makes the residents of his hometown so angry by what he says about God's love for the Gentiles that they take him "to the brow of the hill on which the town was built, in order to throw him off the cliff" to his death (Luke 4:29). Their intent, inspired presumably by the Evil One working in their hearts, was to kill Jesus. But Jesus walks right through the crowd and goes on his way (v. 30).

The next attempt by the cosmic forces that were bent on destroying Jesus was in the form of the raging sea in Mark 4:35–41. After a busy day of preaching, Jesus enters a boat and asks his disciples to go to the other side of the Sea of Galilee. While in the boat, a "furious squall" comes up and threatens to swamp the boat. Jesus is sleeping peacefully in the stern of the boat. Finally, the disciples awake him with the question, "Teacher, don't you care if we drown [lit., 'we are being destroyed']?" The first person plural verb here includes Jesus along with his disciples in this threatened drowning. Jesus then gets up and quiets the wind and the waves.

This storm on the Sea of Galilee is not simply a freak squall but is the work of spiritual forces of evil. In the mythology of the ancient world, the sea is the home of the sea monster, the cosmic Rahab, who is associated with darkness and chaos (see Ps. 74:12–14; 89:9–10; Isa. 27:1; 51:9).[1] "The uncontrollable oceans were associated with hostile powers that threaten life on the inhabited land. This concept is expressed in . . . *Enuma Elish* (also known as The Epic of Creation), in which the god Marduk rose as champion and king of the gods to defeat Tiamat, a goddess of watery chaos."[2] Put in a biblical context, Satan, the prince of darkness, is at work here in the storm on the Sea of Galilee, attempting to destroy Jesus, the Son of Most High God, by capsizing the boat and drowning him.

Two more attempts on the life of Jesus are cited in the gospel of John. One is when the Jewish leadership takes up stones to kill Jesus—first, after Jesus said, "Before Abraham was born, I am" (8:58–59), and the other is after Jesus said, "I and the Father are one" (10:30–31). In both cases, the Jewish leaders charge Jesus with blasphemy, and the Old Testament penalty for blasphemy was death by stoning (Lev. 24:13–16). Jesus, however, as in Luke 4, miraculously eludes their grasp.

The sixth and final time that I propose Jesus faced death during his ministry and prior to his sacrifice on the cross is in the garden of Gethsemane: "A crowd armed with swords and clubs, sent from the chief priests, the teachers of the law, and the elders" comes with Judas to arrest Jesus (Mark 14:43). As they approach, Peter brandishes his weapon and actually cuts off the ear of the servant of the high priest (Luke 22:49–50; John 18:10). What a perfect opportunity for a quick skirmish of self-defense in which the temple guard quickly assassinates Jesus. Jesus, however, defuses the situation immediately by rebuking Peter ("No more of this!"), healing the servant of the high priest, and surrendering without a fight into the hands of his enemies (Luke 22:51–53; John 18:11). His hour to die has now come, and it must be the death on the cross.

That what happens here in the garden of Gethsemane is the work of Satan seems implied from a previous conversation Jesus had with Peter. A few months prior to Gethsemane, Peter had confessed to Jesus, "You are the Christ" (Mark 8:29 NIV). Jesus then outlined for his disciples what was soon going to happen to

him in Jerusalem: his coming rejection, suffering, death, and resurrection. "Peter took [Jesus] aside and began to rebuke him. But
when Jesus turned and looked at his disciples, he rebuked Peter.
'Get behind me, Satan!' he said. 'You do not have in mind the concerns of God, but merely human concerns'" (Mark 8:32–33). We
rightly interpret Jesus' words to mean that any attempt to keep
him from fulfilling his life's work on the cross is the work of Satan.
It is also plausible, however, that Jesus was looking ahead and saw
Peter's attempt to provoke a skirmish in the garden of Gethsemane, in which Jesus could easily be assassinated and thus be pre-
vented from dying on the cross. Such an untimely death likewise
would be the work of Satan.[3]

Why was Satan so intent on destroying Jesus during his childhood and earthly ministry? Because, to begin with, Jesus was intent
on destroying the Devil and his work. There was a war going on.
Moreover, Satan wanted to do everything in his power to prevent
Jesus from dying the only death that would accomplish his life's
mission, namely, our redemption through his death on a cross.[4]

As we saw in chapter 1, Jesus was born to die. But not just
any death would atone for sins; it had to be death on a cross. Paul
explains this clearly in Galatians 3:10–14. Jesus had to die a death
that was connected with the curse of God, which relates to the
fruit of a tree. Therefore, the death of the Redeemer—the first
fruit—must be on a tree/cross. We are all under the curse of God
because of our sin, for as Deuteronomy 27:26 states as quoted by
Paul, "Cursed is everyone who does not continue to do everything
written in the Book of the Law" (Gal. 3:10). Since no one obeys
God's law perfectly, the only way that curse could be broken is for
a perfect person to bear the curse for us—which is what Jesus did
by dying the death of a curse. Satan knew that if he could prevent
Jesus from going to the cross, atonement for sin would never be
made—and the Devil would win the war.

When Jesus was hanging on the cross, many of his enemies taunted and jeered him, hurling insults: "You who are going to destroy the temple and build it in three days, save yourself! Come down from the cross, if you are the Son of God" (Matt. 27:40). There was likely, though, one particular voice in the crowd that was deadly serious—the voice of Satan: "Come down from the cross! Come down from the cross!" If anything, those human voices jeering Jesus at Calvary were, in fact, used by the Devil as a form of reverse psychology, hoping that Jesus would prove himself and manifest his power by coming down from the cross and so failing to fulfill his life's mission.

Did you ever notice that the offer of Jesus' earthly enemies at the foot of the cross is similar to the offer that his spiritual enemy, Satan, made during Jesus' temptations? In his third temptation as recorded in Matthew 4, the Devil "showed him all the kingdoms of the world and their splendor. 'All this I will give you,' he said, 'if you will bow down and worship me'" (vv. 8–9). Satan was offering Jesus a way to become king over all the nations, but in a way that would save him from dying on the cross. This is exactly what the elders, chief priests, and teachers of the law were offering to Jesus three years later as he hung on the cross: "He saved others . . . but he can't save himself! He's the king of Israel! Let him come down now from the cross, and we will believe in him" (Matt. 27:42). If he saved himself from dying by coming down from the cross, they would believe in him as their king. Those doing the taunting, of course, didn't seriously expect that would happen. But one voice *was* serious—the voice of Satan: "Come down from the cross! Come down from the cross!"

The celestial war that began at Christmas did not end until after Jesus' resurrection and ascension. In one of John's visions in the book of Revelation, he saw an enormous red dragon with seven heads and ten horns and seven crowns on its heads (12:3). He was ready to devour the Christ child the moment he was born. But he failed, and the child, the Son of God, "was snatched up to God and to his throne" (v. 5). Reading between the lines, I surmise that the dragon, who is clearly Satan (v. 9), pursued Christ as he was ascending to heaven in order to have one last opportunity to destroy him. This resulted in "war in heaven. Michael and his angels fought against the dragon, and the dragon and his angels fought back. But he was not strong enough, and they lost their place in heaven" (vv. 7–8).

The celestial war was over. Jesus Christ, the Son of God, presented his blood before his Father in the heavenly Most Holy Place, while Michael and his angels gave the final defeat to the Devil and his angels. Jesus had won the war. And let us never forget when that war began in all earnest. The beginning of that celestial war: Christmas.

## CHAPTER 3

# O Little Town of Bethlehem

O little town of Bethlehem, how still we see thee lie!
Above thy deep and dreamless sleep the silent stars go by.
—Phillips Brooks

We sing this song every Christmas, and we likely have a picture in our minds of the little town of Bethlehem. That picture is of a perfect town, a Currier-and-Ives sort of town, nestled in a valley, a picture of pristine peace. This picture is part of our Christmas mythology.

Contemporary Bethlehem, of course, is quite different from biblical Bethlehem. Today it is a city of about thirty thousand people, a town controlled by the Palestinian authority. During the years of the Second Intifada, Bethlehem became a city associated with violence. A group of about two hundred militants hid themselves in the Church of the Nativity for well over a month, and they were only flushed out with violence, resulting in the death of several dozen of them and much damage to the church.

But that's in the twenty-first century, right? Wasn't the Bethlehem of Bible times a town with a reputation of peace and tranquility?

I admit that's the sort of mental picture of Bethlehem I had. It developed during the time when I served my first church, which was in Leighton, Iowa, a small village of less than one hundred fifty people and well off the beaten path. I remember coming into the town on a winter night, traveling on the road from the south. As I crested a small hill, I saw the town sleeping peacefully in the valley. Leighton seemed especially delightful to me because we had moved there during the summer of the racial riots of the late 1960s from a city that had its share of racial tension and unrest.

But a town is known by its history, and that history shapes its reputation. If we mention the names of certain towns or cities today, images of its reputation immediately come to mind. New Orleans. New York. Paris. Las Vegas. Hollywood. Hong Kong. People in Bible times, too, knew the reputations of towns and cities. Sad events or tragic happenings are, of course, associated with almost every biblical town, but Bethlehem seems to have had a greater share of such things. Bethlehem?

Except for its being the boyhood home of David, Bethlehem and the Old Testament stories about it are as far from a sea of tranquility as one can imagine. Indeed, long before the baby Jesus was born there, this small hamlet was already associated with some of the saddest and most tragic events in the Bible. Bethlehem was not a village about which you would say, "I would certainly love to be associated with that town."

The first time Bethlehem is mentioned in the Old Testament is in association with Jacob. Jacob had returned from Laban with his wives and his children and settled for a while in Shechem.

Because of a tragic event that had happened there (mentioned in more detail in the next chapter), Jacob suddenly had to leave with his family. He decided to fulfill a vow he had made years ago to return to Bethel, the place where he had seen a vision of angels as he was running away from Esau (Gen. 28:10–22). After Jacob left Bethel with his wives and children, they moved farther south. His favorite wife, Rachel, was pregnant at the time, and went into labor "still some distance from Ephrath" (Gen. 35:16). Ephrath is another name for Bethlehem, as verse 19 points out.

Rachel's delivery of a son was a difficult one, and in the course of the delivery, she lay at the point of death. Before she died, she named her son Ben-Oni, which means "son of my sorrow." There, close to Bethlehem, Jacob buried his wife Rachel. He renamed his son "Benjamin," which means "son of my right hand," but the grave in which he buried Rachel became part of the folklore of the nation as a place associated with sadness and sorrow.

We know this because the Old Testament prophet Jeremiah reminds us of this story. Jeremiah is, of course, "the weeping prophet," so named because he lived during the time in which the land of God's people was devastated by the Babylonians, when thousands of Jews were killed or taken captive to Babylon, and the city of Jerusalem with its temple was destroyed. Jeremiah pictures the captives being taken on the road from Jerusalem to Bethlehem and trudging past Rachel's burial place. This is what he writes in 31:15:

> A voice is heard in Ramah,
> mourning and great weeping,
> Rachel weeping for her children
> and refusing to be comforted,
> because [her children] are no more.

Here, Ramah—the area of Ephrath and Bethlehem—is once again associated with suffering and great sorrow—with the terrible devastation and suffering of God's people.

The next time after the death of Rachel that we encounter the city of Bethlehem is in those chapters of the book of Judges that we rarely read—the R-rated chapters (Judg. 17–21). Judges 17 begins with a certain Micah living in the hill country of Ephraim. He steals some silver from his mother, but his mother had uttered a curse over the thief, not realizing it was her own son. So Micah returns the silver, and his mother hands some of it to a silversmith, who fashions it into a carved image of a god. Micah makes a shrine for the idol.

Shortly thereafter a Levite "from Bethlehem" leaves that town to look for work and to find a place to stay. He chances to come upon Micah's residence, and Micah offers him room and board and a small stipend as his priest and to serve the enshrined idol god. The Levite accepts the offer. So a man from Bethlehem—a priest, no less—is associated with idolatry.

In the next chapter (Judg. 18), a group of six hundred warriors from the tribe of Dan go out and look for a place to settle, and they explore the very land where Micah and the Levite from Bethlehem are living. They attack the place, steal the idol, and persuade the Levite to become the priest of an entire tribe instead of just one household. The priest—though probably not having a lot of choice—accepts the offer. So now a resident of the town of Bethlehem is associated with idolatry, violence, and opportunism.

In Judges 19 a new story begins about a Levite from the hill country of Ephraim who obtains a concubine from Bethlehem. This woman is unfaithful and returns to her father's house, but the husband returns to Bethlehem to retrieve his concubine. After several days of partying with his father-in-law, the Levite leaves with his woman to head back home. They get as far as Gibeah, about a day's journey, and are invited into the home of an old man for the night. While he was providing for him, some "wicked men of the city" surrounded the house and demanded the old man to hand over to them the Levite "so we can have sex with him" (Judg. 19:22).

Instead, the Levite offers his concubine to the men. During that night the woman is gang-raped, and by dawn is almost dead. The Levite sets her on his donkey and continues his journey, and by the time they arrive in Ephraim, she is dead. So the Levite cuts up this woman from Bethlehem "limb by limb, into twelve parts and sent them into all the areas of Israel" (Judg. 19:29). The end result is a civil war in Israel in which the tribe of Benjamin is almost wiped out (Judg. 20). In this story in Judges, Bethlehem is thus associated with immorality and with violence.

The next story in the Old Testament in which Bethlehem plays a role is the book of Ruth. Elimelech and his wife, Naomi, leave the promised land of Canaan because of a famine and go to the land of Moab. Their two sons marry Moabite women, but in a short time all three of these men die. Naomi decides to return to Bethlehem alone, though Ruth insists on traveling with her. She asks the women of Bethlehem to call her "Mara": "Call me Mara, because the Almighty has made my life very bitter. I went away full, but the LORD has brought me back empty. Why call me Naomi? The LORD has afflicted me; the Almighty has brought misfortune upon me" (Ruth 1:20–21). So once again, Bethlehem in the Old Testament is home to sadness and sorrow, and associated with people who, regardless of God's promise, leave the land God has given to them, trying to find a better future in a pagan land.

It is only by God's grace as he works through the ingenuity and forthrightness of Ruth and Naomi that something positive about Bethlehem is finally recorded in the Scripture. Ruth works in the fields of Bethlehem during the time of the harvest and eventually marries Boaz, a kinsman of Naomi's deceased husband. Together

Ruth and Boaz have a child whom they name Obed, who becomes the grandfather of Israel's greatest king, David.

When we think of the little town of Bethlehem, we usually think of it only as the birthplace of Christ and the ancestral home of David. As we have seen, however, Scripture records far more to the history of Bethlehem, and all of it is connected with either extreme sadness, unfaithfulness, and seedy or despicable behavior. Consider the behavior of even David's family at the time that David was anointed as king. They were content not to trust the choice of God from among their sons but to look on outward appearance. David initially wasn't even at the event during which he was chosen to be anointed as king (1 Sam. 16).

And even in David's own life, we find one more story that does not reflect positively on the little town. During the time that David was hiding in the cave of Adullam, the Philistines had a garrison that controlled Bethlehem. This made David very sad, and he longed for the opportunity to have a drink of water from the well in Bethlehem.

Three of his mighty men decided to fulfill David's wish. They broke through the lines of the Philistines and managed to get to the well of the city of Bethlehem. They filled a jug for David and carried it back to him. "But he refused to drink it; instead, he poured it out before the Lord. 'Far be it from me, Lord, to do this!' he said. 'Is it not the blood of men who went at the risk of their lives?'" (2 Sam. 23:16–17). The sad part about this story is, of course, that Bethlehem had been unable to defend itself and ended up in the hands of the pagan Philistines, the archenemy of Israel.

If a town's reputation is shaped by its history, then Bethlehem's is indeed sordid. God could have chosen to have his Son born in Jerusalem or in Bethel or in some other town that had more positive associations. But God chose to have his Son born in Bethlehem, with all of its secrets and its shady history.

## CHAPTER 4

# Mary's Shame

Mary plays a central role in the Christmas story, beginning with the Advent season. It is with a certain amount of hesitation that I talk about Mary, because she is so revered in many Christian circles. Certainly this is so in many Roman Catholic and Eastern Orthodox circles, but even some Protestant circles show an increasing interest in the blessed Virgin Mary. And in Luke 1—in view of her purity and virginity—the humility demonstrated in her willingness to become the mother of the Christ child is amazing. It fills a person with awe and deep gratitude to see the mystery of God at work in this young woman.

Nevertheless, what is often not recognized in connection with Mary's role in this Christmas story is that Luke 1:26–38 is one of the saddest stories in the Bible. This is especially so when you catch the hints contained in the rest of the Christmas narrative about the effects of her willingness to be God's servant in this most astounding way. As you read the story about the role of Mary and put yourself in her culture and her unique situation, it cannot help but bring tears to your eyes.

The first century was steeped in what is called an "honor-shame culture," though its roots go all the way back to the Old Testament. For that matter, in traditional Middle Eastern cultures it stretches all the way into the twenty-first century A.D. Even today, every now and then news media pick up on severe discipline meted out in a Muslim country that can only be explained by the deeply ingrained honor-shame culture.

It is not my intent to explore all the features of this culture, but we do need to see how it played itself out in the family. Family honor was everything, and a first-century family would do anything to maintain the honor and integrity of the family name. Anything that brought shame to the family needed to be dealt with quickly and without hesitation.

One of the areas that could bring shame to a family was that of sexuality. Genesis 34 offers an excellent example. In that chapter, Shechem, the son of a pagan clan leader, sexually violated Dinah, the daughter of Jacob and Leah. Most scholars argue that the violation was rape—the rape of a virgin, for Dinah was not married. Shechem had forced sexual relations with her, and it had violated the honor of Jacob's clan. Jacob's sons "were filled with grief and fury, because Shechem had done a disgraceful [shameful] thing in Israel" (v. 7 NIV).

In spite of his violating cultural-sexual taboos, Shechem expressed a desire to marry Dinah. As a result, his father, Hamor, paid a visit to Jacob and made a proposal to him. He suggested the two clans begin to intermarry. Regarding Dinah, he was willing to pay whatever bride price was necessary if Jacob would agree to give her in marriage to his son Shechem. Jacob's sons took over the negotiations and insisted that they could not give Dinah to a clan that was not circumcised; "that would be a disgrace to us" (v. 14). Therefore they proposed that the entire clan be circumcised.

All the men of the clan agreed to this proposal and were

circumcised. Three days later, however, when the men of Shechem were still in pain from their circumcision wounds, Simeon and Levi, two of the blood brothers of Dinah, took it upon themselves to attack the unsuspecting city, killing every male, looting the city, and carrying off all the women and the children. They had restored honor to their clan for the shame and disgrace that Shechem had brought through his rape of Dinah.

In secular Western culture of the twenty-first century, sexual relations outside of marriage are a common thing. Huge numbers of babies are born each year to young, single mothers—sometimes as a result of living with a boyfriend, sometimes as a result of a casual sexual relationship. We are no longer shocked by such statistics, and rarely is there any shame involved.

But Mary lived in the first century B.C., when sexual relations outside of marriage did matter, whether the act was forced or consensual—and they were a cause of scandal in the community and shame in the family. After Mary's visit by the angel Gabriel, the Holy Spirit impregnated her. Sooner or later she would have to break the news to her parents that she is pregnant with the Christ child. Let's imagine the conversation as she tells her parents.

"Mom, I'm pregnant."

"What?! You've never left the house. How did this happen? Tell us, who is the father?"

"God is."

"What do you mean, 'God is'? Tell us again, who is the father?"

"Well, an angel came to me and told me I was going to be pregnant with a child who would be 'Son of the Most High.' He said the Holy Spirit would provide the seed."

"Come on, Mary. Get real. That was just a dream. Did you find a way to sneak out of the house and get together with your fiancé, Joseph?"

"No! Joseph had nothing to do with this. It's all about God."

"Mary, how could you do this to us? How could you bring such shame to our family? Don't you realize how people are going to talk once they start noticing things? You were always such a good girl. How could you let this happen?"

That this was a scandal in Mary's home is plain from Matthew 1, for eventually Joseph heard about Mary's pregnancy. Perhaps Mary's parents contacted him to get his side of the story, and he denied vigorously having anything to do with her pregnancy. But the situation did present a real problem for Joseph. If he went through with the marriage, it would be tacitly admitting that he was the father of the baby, and he would share in that shame. The only honorable thing for him to do would be to break the engagement and divorce Mary.

And that is precisely what he decided to do. His only question was whether he would do so quietly or in a public manner, in order "to expose her to public disgrace." That way his honor would be clear to everyone (see Matt. 1:19). As he was puzzling which route to take, "an angel of the Lord" directly intervened. He appeared to Joseph in a dream, and through that encounter Joseph became convinced that Mary's story was true and that he should marry her (vv. 20–21).

Then we read something amazing: "When Joseph woke up, he did what the angel of the Lord had commanded him and took Mary home as his wife" (Matt. 1:24). This does not mean he married her at that time. Luke 2, in fact, clearly indicates that when Joseph and Mary went to Bethlehem, Mary "was pledged to be married to [Joseph]" (v. 5). Joseph and Mary began to live together without being formally married. Matthew 1:25 is careful to state that there was no sexual relationship, and hence no marital relationship between the two of them, until after the birth of Jesus.

That was something virtually unheard of in the ancient world—that a man and a woman would live together before the official, family-sanctioned wedding night. But why wasn't Mary at home with her parents, where every respectable girl stayed until the wedding day? I propose it was because Mary, to put it bluntly, had been kicked out of her home. Her disgrace and shame were unacceptable to her family circle, and her parents could not tolerate her situation. This is sad—truly sad.

In a recent book by Matthew J. Marohl, the author suggests an even more horrendous scenario.[1] It is well known that the issue of premarital purity is vital in traditional Middle Eastern culture even today. Those who cross over the line—or even appear to cross over the line—can end up being killed in what is called an "honor killing,"[2] and the legal framework of such cultures often looks the other direction in regard to such a killing. Marohl has collected a significant amount of evidence that honor killings were openly discussed and even occasionally occurred in the Greco-Roman and Jewish world of the first century.[3] Is it possible that Mary, as soon as her parents found out that she had become pregnant, had to flee her home in order to save her life? I certainly cannot say this definitively, but it's not unreasonable to entertain the suggestion.[4]

That Mary could no longer live at home for whatever reason is confirmed, I believe, in a subsequent story, one that we read so quickly at Christmastime and do not reflect on how it is connected to the larger picture. This story is in Luke 1:39–45, which records Mary's visit to Elizabeth. The trek from Nazareth to the "hill country of Judea" was nearly eighty miles, and there is no record of anyone accompanying Mary on her visit to Elizabeth. She may have traveled, of course, with a group, but she is not brought there by her family.

Why would a single girl travel alone for all that distance? Because she had to live somewhere, and because she knew that, of all the people in the world, Elizabeth would understand. After all, her husband, Zechariah, had also recently been visited by an angel with the promise of a miraculous birth. And now Elizabeth, well beyond her child-bearing years, was pregnant. Elizabeth, then, would accept the pregnant virgin Mary and would believe her story. This may, in fact, be the reason why the angel Gabriel specifically told Mary that Elizabeth was going to have a child (v. 36). Note that Mary stayed there about three months, from the time that Elizabeth was in her sixth month until just before John's birth (vv. 36, 56).

But where did Mary go after she left Elizabeth? She still had six months to go before the birth of her son, Jesus. I believe that by this time Joseph had struggled with the issue of what to do, had received his dream, and had made his decision to eventually wed Mary, regardless of the shame it would bring to him. I suggest, then, that he went to Elizabeth and Zechariah's at the end of Mary's first three months in order to bring her back with him to Nazareth. And if the possibility of an honor killing is at all a part of this picture, Joseph also had the role of protecting Mary 24/7, thus fulfilling the commitment he made to be obedient to "what the angel of the Lord had commanded him" (Matt. 1:24).

The story of the trip that Joseph and Mary took to Bethlehem just before Jesus' birth appears to confirm this scenario. From Nazareth to Bethlehem was about a hundred miles, a distance that would take a minimum of six days, if not more. I have often asked women who have experienced pregnancy and childbirth how they would feel about walking on dusty roads, up and down hills for six days—a week before they were ready to give birth. Usually these women gasp at the thought.

Maybe Mary didn't have to walk—at least, the Christmas pictures we're so familiar with show her riding on a donkey. So I ask these same women whether they would like to be jounced around on a donkey for six days just before the time of delivery. Riding on a donkey is not like riding in a Cadillac! The reaction of these same women is no less aghast than with the idea of walking.

And the plot gets even thicker when you realize that, from Mary's standpoint, going to Bethlehem for the census was not necessary. We in the United States are used to a census every ten years, by which the government determines population and sociological trends. A census is also important for establishing the boundaries of legislative districts for a government that is a constitutional republic.

In the ancient world, however, a census was taken for only two reasons: One was for military purposes, to see how many men of warrior age a king could count on for his army (see 2 Sam. 24). The other reason was for taxation purposes, so that the ruler could estimate how much taxes he could collect for his palaces and other grand spending ventures. Mary, of course, was not a male, and I doubt if she had any independent income. There was no reason for her to participate in the census.

Admittedly, the NIV reads this way: "So Joseph also went up from the town of Nazareth in Galilee to Judea, to Bethlehem the town of David, because he belonged to the house and line of David. He went there to register with Mary, who was pledged to be married to him and was expecting a child" (Luke 2:4–5). It may sound here as if both Joseph and Mary needed to go to Bethlehem to register together. I suggest, however, that the comma belongs in a different place: "And Joseph also went up from Galilee, from the city of Nazareth, to Judea, to the city of David (called Bethlehem)—because he was of the house and lineage of David—to register; [he went] with Mary, the one pledged to be married to him, being pregnant."[5] The amended text emphasizes Mary's travel with Joseph, not her registration with Joseph. Even if by some chance husbands and wives did need to register together in this particular census, that would not apply to Mary and Joseph since they were not yet legally married.

If Mary did not have to be in Bethlehem, why then did she trek all the way there with Joseph? Because Joseph, being male and having a carpentry business, had to go, and because he had no safe place to leave Mary. Her family had apparently rejected her. Joseph was the *only one* other than Elizabeth who accepted the truth about her story, and it was his task to care for his fiancée and protect her. When I think of Joseph and Mary trudging the dusty roads of Galilee, Samaria, and Judea to go to Bethlehem, with Mary stopping often because she simply couldn't walk another step or ride another inch, it pains my heart.

Moreover, the grammar of the phrases used to describe Mary in Luke 2:5 suggests this scenario. An expanded translation of this verse would go something like this: "[Joseph also went to the town of Bethlehem] to enroll himself, accompanied by Mary, the one who was engaged to him, because [*or, although*] she was with child."[6] In other words, Mary accompanies Joseph to Bethlehem *because* she is pregnant out of wedlock, and Joseph has agreed in his dream to take care of her when no one else would; or *although* she is pregnant and, certainly then, should not have been traveling a hundred miles in her state.

Did Mary have any inkling of what lay ahead for her when she said to the angel, "May it be to me as you have said" (Luke 1:38 NIV)? Perhaps some. We certainly do not get the feeling that she jumped for joy at the chance to be the mother of the Christ child, and she undoubtedly knew the traditions of her culture for girls who became pregnant before being married. But she may have been unaware of the full extent of the rejection she would experience. What Isaiah prophesied about the Servant of the Lord is indeed true in its fulfillment: "He was despised and rejected by men" (Isa. 53:3 NIV). That rejection began even before he was born. Or listen to what the apostle John says in his prologue about the Word: "He came to that which was his own, but his own did not receive him" (John 1:11). In the context of his gospel, John probably has the Jewish people in mind, but that rejection began with "his own" family prior to Jesus' birth. In chapter 6 we will see further evidence of the rejection of Jesus by the extended Davidic family.

Mary's story is indeed a sad and lonely one. During her pregnancy, only two people believed her story: Elizabeth and Joseph. We applaud Mary because of her willingness to let her womb be used to carry to term the Son of the Most High, the Messiah, the promised coming king of Israel. But there was no applause in Nazareth when that event began. And as the story played itself out during the nine months of Mary's pregnancy, tears must have often filled her eyes.

## CHAPTER 5

# Mary's Song—and Zechariah's

This book is about the painful, not-so-silent night of Christmas. As you've probably gathered by now, there are two separate elements to this story. One is that Christmas is the beginning of war, not the establishment of peace. It is the beginning of war in the celestial sphere, where Christ came into the world to destroy the Devil, and the Devil reciprocated by trying to destroy Christ. But that war took place here on earth, as the Devil attempted in various ways to kill Jesus and thus not let him get to the cross, his divinely appointed sacrifice for human sin. The other painful element is that, for the most prominent characters, their side to the story holds an incredible sadness and tragedy. When we look closely at what is happening to Mary and Joseph in particular, it brings tears to one's eyes.

The previous chapter dealt with the shame that Mary had to bear by becoming pregnant out of wedlock, especially when she couldn't convince her parents, or her fiancé, Joseph, of how she had become pregnant. The only one who seemed to understand was her elderly and pregnant relative Elizabeth, and so Mary went to visit her for three months immediately after the annunciation. When Mary entered Elizabeth's home, the baby John moved inside the womb of Elizabeth, and she burst out in a blessing for Mary. According to Luke 1, Mary in turn responded by singing a song, which now goes by the title the *Magnificat*, so named because in the Latin Vulgate translation, *magnificat* is the first word of the song: "My soul glorifies [or magnifies] the Lord" (v. 46).

One would think that in her song, Mary would express some of the wonder of what was happening inside her body, even though everyone else seemed to be ashamed of her. Or that she might express some joy that her relative Elizabeth understood her feelings of frustration and her pain over the loss of social acceptance. And she does express joy that God has been mindful of her and that when all is said and done, she will be vindicated: "From now on all generations will call me blessed" (v. 48).

Unfortunately, that is about all we usually notice about the song—how excited Mary seems in the first three verses. But when you look at the rest of the song, you realize quickly that this is primarily a song of conflict and war—and of God's power to vindicate those who are trodden down, both in her immediate present and in Israel's more distant past. Mary's song is about the mighty warrior God, whose sovereign plan of history will always emerge victorious. It's as if she were saying, "In this conflict between my Son and Satan, my Son will come out the victor."

In Luke 1:49, the war imagery is called up when Mary calls God "the Mighty One." This expression uses a term that is ascribed to the warrior God in Psalm 24:8: "Who is this King of glory? The LORD strong and *mighty*, the LORD *mighty* in battle." One of the standard names used for Israel's God in the Old Testament is "the

*Mighty arm of God*
*Peaceful Warrior*

Mighty One of Jacob" (e.g., Gen. 49:24; Ps. 132:2, 5; Isa. 49:26; 60:16). As Tremper Longman and Daniel Reid argue in their book about God as a warrior, "Luke, in the *Magnificat*, has . . . drawn our attention to the renewed activity of the 'Mighty One' (*ho dynatos*) who had performed mighty deeds with his arm."[1]

What are these deeds that the Mighty One has performed "with his arm" (Luke 1:51)? The clue is in the word *arm*, which is used for the first time in the Old Testament in connection with God's promise to Moses that he will lead the Israelites "out from under the yoke of the Egyptians . . . I will redeem you with an outstretched arm and with mighty acts of judgment" (Exod. 6:6). Indeed, after the Israelites had crossed the Red Sea and were singing their song of victory, they included these words: "terror and dread will fall on [the people of Canaan]. By the power of your arm they will be as still as a stone" (15:16). Throughout the book of Deuteronomy (4:34; 5:15; 7:19; 11:2; 26:8; cf. 9:29), references to God's "mighty hand and outstretched arm" run like a refrain. That this remained part of the phraseology of the exodus is evident in Paul's message in Antioch of Pisidia, when he testified that God led his people out of Egypt (lit.) "with an uplifted arm," performing mighty deeds on behalf of his people (Acts 13:17; cf. 7:36).

A further military phrase of the *Magnificat* occurs when Mary refers to those whom God has "scattered" (Luke 1:51). The verb *scattered* that occurs here is used in the Old Testament when talking about the idea of scattering, both for the scattering of God's enemies (e.g., Num. 10:35; 2 Sam. 22:15; Ps. 18:14; 68:1, 14; 89:10) and, even more common, for the scattering among the nations of God's people in judgment (e.g., Ps. 44:11; Isa. 11:12; Jer. 23:2; Ezek. 11:16; 20:34, 41; Joel 3:2). The warrior God is a powerful God, who scatters people as he wills with his mighty hand.

In Luke 1:52–53 we encounter obvious references to God as a warrior king of all the earth: "He has brought down rulers from their thrones [and] . . . has sent the rich away empty." In the construction that Mary uses here—technically called a chiasm—the "rulers" and the "rich" refer to essentially the same people; wealth, after all, brings power. God has no use for those who assert their power on a human level and take advantage of the weak. By contrast, he promises to act mightily to champion the cause of those who have no power themselves, "the humble" and "the hungry," to be merciful to them, and to remember his covenant with Abraham.

While the exodus from Egypt does serve as a historical event for some of the military expressions here, there is more going on in this song. Most of the conflict that Mary sings about seems not to be linked to any specific events in the history of the Old Testament. For the most part, then, Mary is talking in general about God's actions of war. If anything, in the context of the gospel of Luke, the references in this song describe the ministry of Jesus both in his earthly life and in his reign from heaven: who "lifted up the humble . . . filled the hungry with good things . . . [and] sent the rich away empty." Some prominent evangelical scholars suggest that the verbs used in this song are more prophetic in nature, portraying "the ultimate . . . events tied to Jesus' final victory. These events are seen as so certain that, even though they are future events, they can be portrayed as past realities."[2] Mary, in other words, sees God's ultimate victory over the powers of evil that comes through the work of his Son as he scatters the proud—those who treat their fellow humans with contempt and with a view to their own interests.

Mary is not the only one, however, to present images of conflict. In Luke 1, after the birth of John the Baptist and in particular at his circumcision, God opens the mouth of his father, Zechariah. Zechariah also sings a song, one that is traditionally called the *Benedictus*. Like Mary's song, it too is filled with military imagery. In Luke 1:69, Zechariah sings that God has "raised up a horn of salvation for us." *Horn* has numerous meanings in English, among them, something sticking out of an animal's head, like the horns on a bull. As the NIV text note says on this verse, "*Horn* here symbolizes strength," just as the bull symbolizes strength. The specific phrase "horn of salvation" is drawn from one of the songs of David, Israel's greatest military king: "The LORD is my rock, my fortress and my deliverer; my God is my rock, in whom I take refuge, my shield and the horn of my salvation, my stronghold" (Ps. 18:2; cf. 2 Sam. 22:3).

Psalm 18 is filled, in fact, with battlefield imagery from the life of David. The words "fortress," "refuge," "shield," and "stronghold" are all military words. Moreover, animal horns were used to symbolize strength, sometimes with connotations of military victory (see Deut. 33:17; Ps. 92:9–11). Note, too, Psalm 132:17, where God promises to strengthen the dynasty of David: "Here I will make a horn grow for David and set up a lamp for my anointed one."

In Luke 1:71, the military metaphor is further evident where Zechariah sings about "salvation from our enemies." The words *salvation* and *save* are frequently used in the Old Testament to refer to the power of Yahweh as the warrior God, who rescues his people from their enemies. In Psalm 74:12–13, for instance, God is the King who "brings salvation on the earth . . . who split open the sea by your power; you broke the heads of the monster in the waters." In terms of ancient mythology, this monster represented the powers of chaos, the power of the underworld; in biblical theology, it refers to the power of Satan.

Another example of salvation used in terms of war appears in Psalm 60:11–12, where the psalmist acknowledges that "the help [salvation] of man is worthless. With God we will gain the victory, and he will trample down our enemies" (NIV cf. also Ps. 144:10). Zechariah, the father of John the Baptist, echoes this theme of deliverance in Luke 1:74, where he refers to God's oath to Abraham "to rescue us from the hand of our enemies, and to enable us to serve him without fear."

The focus of Zechariah's song is, of course, the role of his son in this ongoing battle that the Messiah will wage against the forces of evil. John is to go before the Lord Jesus to prepare the way for him (Luke 1:76); that is, he is to prepare the way for the one who will receive the throne of his ancestor David (1:32). The main role of an ancient king was to lead his people in battle and to defeat all enemies. Thus, John's task is to tell God's people about this coming king and to teach them about their coming salvation, their coming rescue (1:77).

One cannot read the last part of Zechariah's song without thinking of Isaiah 9:2–7. There, the prophet refers to "people walking in darkness . . . in the land of the shadow of death," because of "the yoke that burdens them, the bar across their shoulders, the rod of their oppressor" (vv. 2, 4 NIV). But to them comes "a great light," who enlarges the nation and increases their joy, because the oppressor is thrown off. And who is this One? "To us a child is born, to us a son is given, and the government will be on his shoulders. And he will be called Wonderful Counselor, Mighty God, Everlasting Father, Prince of Peace. Of the increase of his government and peace there will be no end. He will reign on David's throne and over his kingdom . . . forever" (vv. 6–7). Zechariah picks up this imagery of the victorious king as he sings, "because of the tender mercy of our God, by which the rising sun will come to us from heaven to shine on those living in darkness and in the shadow of death, to guide our feet into the path of peace" (Luke 1:78–79).

True, there is more to the songs of Mary and Zechariah than simply expressing war imagery. Mary glorifies God and sings of his mercy extended to those who fear him. Zechariah exalts the fact that God has shown mercy to Israel's ancestors and has remembered his covenant promises. But if we skim quickly over the last half of these songs or even further dilute understanding by hearing them sung in Latin, we will miss their strong element of military imagery. It is Christmastime, and war is beginning. That war will be long, and there will be many skirmishes and battles between Jesus and Satan. But the outcome is secure: through the mercy of God, the end result will be peace. That peace, however, lies not in the present but in the future.

## CHAPTER 6

# The *Katalyma*

I n the preceding chapter, we left Joseph and Mary as they were on their way to Bethlehem because of the census ordered by Caesar Augustus. As I suggested in chapter 4, the pregnant Mary did not really have to go to Bethlehem because, as a young girl, she most likely did not have any independent income for taxation, neither would she have been a candidate for the military—the two purposes for an ancient census. But in the case that Mary had been rejected by her immediate family because of her pregnancy, Joseph had little choice but to take his fiancée along. Once they arrived in Bethlehem, the situation did not get any better. In fact, it got worse.

Here is what we read in the familiar Christmas story: "While they were there, the time came for the baby to be born, and she gave birth to her firstborn, a son. She wrapped him in cloths and placed him in a manger, because there was no room for them in the inn" (Luke 2:6–7 NIV).

I suspect that when most of us read the word *inn* we conjure up an image of the twenty-first-century versions of lodging we're more familiar with. We may unconsciously insert before "inn" the word *Holiday* or *Days* or *Ramada*. Maybe even *Hilton*. All of our Christmas pageants, after all, have a character known as "the inn-keeper," who keeps track of which rooms in his hotel are empty. His (or her) only role is to say, "Sorry, no room in the inn." Once again, however, a knowledge of the customs and culture of New Testament times points us in a different direction.

First, widespread travel was not common in the ancient world, certainly not as common as it is today. Few communities outside of the larger cities such as Jerusalem would have boasted temporary lodging for travelers. Even today, in our mobile society, hotels and inns are still not usually found in small hamlets like Bethlehem, which Micah 5:2 suggests was too small a village even to be on a map.

A large group of "relatives and friends" like those in Luke 2:44 who were returning from the Passover in Jerusalem—and it had to be a large group for Joseph and Mary not to notice that Jesus was not with their company—likely slept under the stars or, at best, in some sort of temporary, portable shelter. To use a modern term, they camped.

Consider this as well. The average person could cover up to fifteen miles per day, and the city of Jerusalem was the usual desti-nation for many travelers. Travelers would plan each day's journey so as to arrive in Jerusalem in late afternoon. Thus, whatever inns may have been available would have been located approximately fifteen miles away from the holy city, not six or seven miles, the distance of Jerusalem from Bethlehem. Any hotel business in Bethlehem would have gone broke before it got off the ground.

Second, when people traveled in the ancient world, the normal thing was to stay with acquaintances, friends, friends of friends, and especially relatives. Let me use an analogy from the data we do have in the New Testament. The New Testament church formed a family, the family or household of God (cf. Gal. 6:10; Eph. 2:19; 1 Tim. 3:5, 15; 1 Peter 4:17). Believers in Christ were considered to be brothers and sisters. We know, too, that when Christians traveled from one community to another, they expected to be welcomed into one of the homes of a "family" member (3 John 8).

Furthermore, note this statement from *The Didache*, an early Christian church order of sorts from the late first or early second century: "But let every one that comes in the name of the Lord be received; and then when you have tested him, you will know him . . . If the one who comes is a traveler, assist him, so far as you are able; but he shall not stay with you more than two or three days" (*Did.* 12). The basis assumed here for extending hospitality to spiritual brothers and sisters was the practice of assisting physical family members as they were traveling.

Joseph is, of course, headed to Bethlehem, the home of his ancestors. It is the town in which he is required to register for the census. Presumably he has relatives living there, even if they are only shirttail relatives of the family of David. According to ancient customs, he would expect to be able to stay in the home of such a relative. That would be the logical place for him to go, not to some temporary lodging hotel (even if Bethlehem had such a business).

This is precisely the implication of Luke 2:7, in the word that has almost universally been translated "inn." The Greek word used is *katalyma*. This word occurs only three times in the New Testament—Mark 14:14; Luke 2:7; 22:11—and denotes the "guest room" that Jesus asked Peter and John to locate in order to make ready the Passover for him and his disciples later that evening. The *katalyma* was undoubtedly a room in a person's home—a room that was probably not in general use except for special occasions. Note that the TNIV translates *katalyma* as "guest room."

I should note that Koine—the Greek of the New Testament

era—did have a word to express a temporary, overnight lodging place for travelers—the word *pandocheion*. Luke is well aware of this word, and his use of it is the only time it appears in the New Testament. In the parable of the good Samaritan, Luke writes that the Samaritan took the wounded traveler to a *pandocheion* ("an inn") and paid the innkeeper for his care (10:34).[1]

I suggest, therefore, that the *katalyma*, the place where Joseph and Mary attempted to find temporary lodging in Bethlehem, was in a house, not in a business. And in keeping with the customs and expectation of the first century, this house was most likely the house of a relative of Joseph—someone, like him, in the lineage of David. He had every reason to expect that, according to ancient family hospitality, lodging would be offered to him by these relatives.

But the *katalyma* was filled with other relatives, as we might expect, for they, too, had come to Bethlehem to register for the census. Now one might suppose that these relatives would nevertheless have made a place for them. They would have seen the state of Mary's pregnancy, would have known that, whether or not labor had started by this time, Mary needed a place to rest after the long, dusty journey, and should have been more than ready to offer her a place in the *katalyma*. But they didn't. They didn't make any room. Why not?

The answer lies in my assertion in chapter 4. Word had spread among the relatives about Mary's unsavory pregnancy and the shame it was bringing to the family name. It's easy to imagine such a gathering of relatives in the *katalyma* of that Bethlehem house, their talking about the latest family gossip, especially the pregnancy of that young girl Mary and Joseph's decision to marry her. Then who should suddenly knock on the door but Joseph and Mary! Imagine the hush that suddenly fell over that gathering of relatives—and the dilemma of what to do! They certainly could not welcome someone who had brought such shame to their family into their midst. That would imply some endorsement of her situation. Luke has it correct: there was no room for Joseph and Mary in the *katalyma*. The family would not hear of it!

The solution? Let them use the place where the animals lodged, which, according to what we know about some ancient houses, may have been an animal shelter attached to that house, or else perhaps a cave somewhere in the back of the property. If nothing else, that would send a message to the couple about what the family thought of their situation. Joseph and Mary were fit only to sleep in the barn with the animals.

Once again, we cannot help but think of the unborn Babe in terms of Isaiah 53:3—that the coming Servant of the Lord "was despised and rejected by men, a man of sorrows, and familiar with suffering. Like one from whom men hide their faces he was despised, and we esteemed him not" (NIV). Or consider again John 1:11: "He came to that which was his own, but his own did not receive him." The rejection of God's Messiah occurred, then, even before he was born. This Son of David was being rejected, it seems, by those who should have received him gladly, namely, his own relatives.

There was pain in Bethlehem on Christmas night. There was rejection in Bethlehem. We today stand by the manger and marvel and rejoice at the Child born to Mary in a barn. "Joy to the world, the Lord is come," we sing. But on that first Christmas night there were no doubt tears in the eyes of Joseph and Mary. Nobody in their family circle would help them. Nobody cared. The only ones who did come to the manger to witness the child were the lowly night-watch shepherds, directed there by God himself, while the prim and proper—yes, and self-righteous—relatives were right upstairs, missing the most awesome birth in the history of the human race. How incredibly sad!

## CHAPTER 7

# The Humiliation of Jesus' Birth

When I think about the dark side of Christmas, and especially about the familiar birth story of Jesus in Luke 2, one word comes to mind: "humiliation." This is not, of course, the only element in the story. There is also a sense of the spectacular—the awesome birth of God's one and only Son, the angel who appears on the fields of Bethlehem surrounded by the brilliant glory of the Lord, and the whole sky filled with an enormous gathering of angels singing a song of praise to some shepherds on the fields of Bethlehem. These are familiar scenes that we emphasize every year in December, and they don't need to be retold here.

But there is a sad, heavy side to this story, a side that we rarely, if ever, think about. That is the side that I'll explore with you in this chapter.

Systematic theologians have traditionally discussed the two states of the incarnate Christ: his state of humiliation and his state of exaltation. A number of steps are concerned in each of these states, as expressed in the Apostles' Creed: his state of humiliation involves his virgin conception, his birth, his life of suffering, his unjust trials before the high priest and before Pilate, his death and burial, and his so-called descent into hell, about which there are many different interpretations. His state of exaltation involves his resurrection, his ascension, his sitting down at God's right hand, and his still-future coming again.

Regarding the first of these two states, humiliation, how often do we pause to consider just how much humiliation is involved in the Christmas story?

Let's begin our analysis with the place where Jesus came from—his throne in heaven. Revelation 4 gives a picture of what that throne room of heaven looks like at the present time. In Revelation 4:1, John is invited by a voice sounding like a trumpet to glimpse what heaven looks like, and here is what he sees. A rainbow, resembling an emerald, encircles God's throne. Surrounding it are various creatures dressed in white, with crowns of gold on their heads. From the throne come flashes of dazzling lightning. And before the throne is a sea of glass, clear as crystal (4:3–6). The scene in this chapter continues with a sampling of the glorious songs that are sung around this throne, honoring the holiness, majesty, and power of the triune God.

This is a picture of absolute, antiseptic cleanliness—of one place that is not touched regularly by the filth of human sin. This is the abode of the holy Trinity. This is where Jesus, the baby of Bethlehem, came from. This is what he left in order to live in this sin-filled earth with all its ugliness. Can we even begin to fathom the humiliation that this change of location involved for God's Son? It would be like our leaving the most gorgeous palace ever built on earth, where we sleep on silk sheets, eat from gold dishes, and dress in designer clothes, to take up residence in the garbage dump of a Third World country. And he came not just for an investigative junket, like a president making a half-day visit to a hurricane-devastated area. He came *to live*! His glorious home in heaven is what Jesus gave up in order to be born as a human being.

Moreover, consider the humiliation of his physical makeup. Jesus left the throne as God the Son, the second person of the Trinity through whom everything was made (John 1:3), and he came to be born as a helpless human being. No person is more helpless than a newborn infant. A baby has no ability to get his own food or drink. She has no ability to find a decent place to sleep. He has no ability to clean himself if he heeds the call of nature. Her only means of making needs known is to cry. While we may sing, "the little Lord Jesus, no crying he makes," it really wasn't so. A baby who doesn't cry isn't normal, and Jesus was a normal infant. A newborn is totally dependent on other human beings for survival. For someone who was with the Father and the Spirit, participating in the creation of the world as the Word of God, that's humiliation! As the apostle Paul said,

> [Christ Jesus], being in very nature God,
>> did not consider equality with God
>> something to be grasped,
> but made himself nothing,
>> taking the very nature of a servant,
>> being made in human likeness.
> And being found in appearance as a man,
>> he *humbled himself* . . .
>> (Phil. 2:5–8 NIV, italics added)

But there is more. As we surmised in the last chapter, Mary and Joseph were not permitted to stay in the guest room, the *katalyma*, of some relative's home in Bethlehem. Rather, they were relegated to the living quarters of the household animals. And let me assure you, the conditions of that "barn" or "stable" were terrible in and of themselves, and especially so when you think of where Jesus had come from.

It is typical to put out a nativity scene at Christmastime. I put one on our mantel each Christmas, and each year I put on fresh, clean straw. Every crèche I have seen is immaculate. Some churches even use live nativity scenes, with live animals. During such an event, I've never seen one animal dirty the stable, but I'm sure if one did, in addition to several "Eeuuwws" coming from the kids, a clean shovel would have quickly removed any bit of bodily waste. After all, we cannot have our nativity scenes dirty, can we?

By contrast, the place where the baby Jesus was born was absolutely filthy. Clean, white-washed barns are a product of the twentieth century, not of the first century B.C. Cow manure and donkey dung must have been everywhere in the birthing room of our Savior. And the flies and perhaps even maggots were everywhere as well.

Let's think of Mary going into labor. From what we read in the New Testament, there was no midwife around. It was just Mary and Joseph. Questions abound in my mind about this scene. Had Joseph ever participated in a birth event before? Probably not. Did he have surgical gloves on? No. Did he have sterilized scissors with which to cut the umbilical cord? No. And if the manger in which Jesus was laid was a small feeding trough, where did Mary lie during labor? Could it have been any other place besides the floor of that stinking barn? If I had been there, would I have held my nose because of the stench?

The gospel of John says that Jesus came to shine into darkness (1:4–5). At nighttime in an era without electricity, what light did Joseph have? At best, only a single oil lamp, with a single wick. It was bad enough for Jesus simply to be born as a human being, worse yet in a filthy, sin-infested world. In addition, he was born in one of the most dark and dismal settings humanly imaginable. Not long before, he was in that shining throne room with the sea of glass all around, clear as crystal, surrounded by choirs singing powerful songs of praise and wearing bright white robes. Now this! It's the shaded side of Christmas we don't like to think about. It's the dark side of Christmas we don't display in our Christmas nativity sets.

In the previous chapter I suggested that the Davidic relatives of Joseph and Mary were in the immediate vicinity, upstairs in the *katalyma*. Perhaps they even heard the labor cries of Mary that came from the barn. Here was a young girl giving birth to her firstborn, and who may have witnessed other births but undoubtedly had no labor and delivery classes. "Serves her right," they probably muttered to each other. They missed the event.

But God would not have the event totally without witnesses, so he sent his angel to announce the birth of the "Savior . . . Christ the Lord" to some shepherds on the fields of Bethlehem, "keeping watch over their flocks at night" (Luke 2:8, 11 NIV). In the Old Testament, the shepherding theme is frequently mentioned. God is a shepherd (e.g., Ps. 23:1), and he took his servant David away from his flocks "to be the shepherd of his people Jacob . . . and David shepherded them with integrity of heart" (Ps. 78:70–72).

It appeared to be an honorable and noble analogy to use. The New Testament uses this Old Testament imagery as well (as in John 10).

Nevertheless, the job of shepherd was not viewed with great awe and wonder in the first century. Craig Keener summarizes the attitude of first-century people toward shepherds:

> God reveals his Son's birth to shepherds, members of a despised and lowly profession (2:8), people who might never be admitted directly to Caesar's court. . . .

It may surprise us that these shepherds would be looked down on by Luke's contemporaries . . . for the most part urban people in the empire viewed shepherds as low class; they appear in lists of professions apt to be uneducated and crude. . . . To some degree, fault lines between white-collar and blue-collar workers in our culture may convey the sense; images of uneducated field workers or herders in other parts of the world might drive home even better the sense of innate superiority some groups of people feel when they compare themselves with others.[1]

Let's realize that the Lord God could have chosen any group to which to announce the birth of his Son. He could have chosen a group of rabbis or scribes in Jerusalem, only a few miles away. He could have chosen the mayor of Bethlehem. He could even have appeared to the relatives in the *katalyma*, telling them to get their act together. But he appeared to those who were lowly and despised. When the shepherds left the manger and "spread the word concerning what had been told them about this child" (Luke 2:17), I doubt if anyone took them seriously: "Well, okay, whatever!"

In the message that the angel gave to the shepherds, he cited the "sign" that would clue the shepherds that they had found the right child: "'This will be a sign for you: you will find a child wrapped in bands of cloth and lying in a manger.' . . . So they went with haste and found Mary and Joseph, and the child lying in the manger" (Luke 2:12, 16 NRSV). What this tells us is that the God-given "sign" of the Christ child at Christmastime is the sign of his humiliation. The shepherds would identify the child because he would be lying in a manger—the feeding trough for animals—an unusual crib for any newborn child regardless of the century.

Furthermore, he would be wrapped in "bands of cloth." That the baby Jesus was wrapped in strips of cloth was not as unusual as was his lying in the manger. Many first-century children were wrapped in cloths after birth. The bands of cloth are comparable to our receiving blankets. To be wrapped tightly in these cloths gave a child a sense of security and comfort. Mary and Joseph used what they had undoubtedly taken along "just in case," and the shepherds could see that, while this child was born in the most abject of circumstances, he was obviously loved and cared for. God saw to that!

Nevertheless, for the Son of God, what a contrast in the nature of his clothing! The Old Testament clearly testifies to the clothing worn by the holy, majestic, triune God: "LORD my God . . . you are clothed with splendor and majesty. The LORD wraps himself in light as with a garment" (Ps. 104:1–2); "The LORD reigns, he is robed in majesty; the LORD is robed in majesty and armed with strength" (Ps. 93:1). Now the Son of God is born in Bethlehem, and he goes from being clothed with light and majesty to being surrounded by darkness, dirt, and defecation, "wrapped in cloths" (Luke 2:7 NIV). As already noted, this enormous decline in the quality of his clothing is part of the "sign" given to the shepherds to help them identify the baby.[2]

In the broader message of the Gospels, these bands of cloth also call to mind another cloth that eventually enwrapped Jesus. When his body was taken down from the cross and laid in a tomb, Joseph of Arimathea "wrapped it in linen cloth and placed it in a tomb cut in the rock" (Luke 23:53). Or, as John writes, Joseph of Arimathea, along with Nicodemus, took the body of Jesus and "wrapped it, with the spices, in strips of linen. This was in accordance with Jewish burial customs" (19:40). Though the Greek words are different, the net effect at his birth and at his burial is the same: Jesus wrapped in cloth.

As we noted in chapter 1, from the moment of Jesus' birth, an aura of death was in the air. The shadow of the cross hung over the manger. Now we see that same theme within the Christmas story in Luke 2. This baby, in these humiliating circumstances, was born to die.

## CHAPTER 8

# The Angels on the Field of Bethlehem

One of the most familiar elements of the Christmas story in Luke 2 is the appearance of the angel to the shepherds. That angel was soon joined by a "great company of the heavenly host . . . praising God and saying, 'Glory to God in the highest, and on earth peace to men on whom his favor rests'" (Luke 2:13–14 NIV). I doubt if there is anyone who does not envision this scene as a huge company of angels dressed in choir robes, perhaps complete with sopranos, altos, tenors, and basses, singing praise to the newborn king and accompanied perhaps by a highly polished heavenly orchestra.

Our Christmas carols reflect this scene.

+ The second stanza of "O Come, All Ye Faithful": "Sing, *choirs of angels*, sing in exultation."
+ The first stanza of "Angels We Have Heard on High": "Angels we have heard on high, *sweetly singing* o'er the plains."

✦ The second line in "It Came upon the Midnight Clear": ". . . from angels bending near the earth to touch their *harps of gold*."
✦ The familiar "Hark, the *herald angels* sing, 'Glory to the newborn king.'"

I, too, have always had this picture in my mind. It's the way every Christmas pageant I can recall has portrayed this scene. But a couple of years ago, I decided to revisit this passage in Luke 2, reading it in the Greek New Testament to see if there was something I may have missed. In doing so, I discovered something I had never realized before and something that is rarely mentioned and never discussed in detail in commentaries on Luke. This passage fits in with one of the two main themes I have been exploring in this book, namely, that Christmas is the beginning of war.

Where is the military imagery in Luke 2:13? Listen carefully: The word that Luke uses for "host" is the Greek word *stratia*, a word that in classical Greek almost invariably denotes an army or a company of soldiers. On occasion the word could be used as an alternate for the Greek word *strateia*, which denotes a military expedition. In either case, the word has strong military connotations.

As I just noted, this Greek word is all but ignored in the commentaries on Luke's gospel. True, some commentators do realize that *stratia* is there. What the NIV translates as "heavenly host," Luke Timothy Johnson translates as "the heavenly army."[1] Christopher Evans refers to the "angels as the divine soldiery,"[2] and F. L. Godet calls them a "troop of angels."[3] The NRSV has a footnote by the word "host" and indicates that in Greek this word means "army." But while these sources do acknowledge the meaning of *stratia*, they do not explore how this military imagery intersects with the Christmas story and with the subsequent life of the babe of Bethlehem.

Most commentators, however, understand this word as a large choir. John Nolland, for example, refers to the "angelic chorus."[4] Joel Green similarly calls the *stratia* "the angelic choir."[5] Darrell Bock goes so far as to suggest that the "angelic praise serves the same function literarily for Luke as do choruses in Greek dramas," who supplied commentary on what was happening in the main story.[6] I believe these commentaries are missing the point. No one to my knowledge has probed deeply what the *stratia* is and what its implications are for the life and ministry of Jesus in the New Testament.

The meaning of many Greek words in the New Testament is, of course, heavily shaped by the Septuagint, the Greek version of the Old Testament. We especially need to rely on the Septuagint when a particular word is used as infrequently in the New Testament as *stratia* is, namely, twice—here and in Acts 7:42, where Stephen in his speech to the Synagogue of the Freedmen refers to Israel's idolatrous history as worshiping "the host of heaven" (NRSV). So let me turn to a quick survey of the twenty-eight uses of *stratia* in the Greek Old Testament.

The majority of these usages (nineteen, to be exact) refers to human armies. For example, *stratia* is used for Pharaoh's army at the time of Israel's exodus from Egypt (Exod. 14:4, 9, 17), for David's army (2 Sam. 3:23; 18:16), for Israel's army (Num. 10:28; Deut. 20:9; 1 Chron. 12:14; 28:1), and for the Assyrian army (2 Chron. 32:9).

The remaining nine uses of *stratia* in the Septuagint refer, like the uses of the term in Luke 2:13 and Acts 7:42, to nonphysical hosts. Here are the passages: 1 Kings 22:19; 2 Chronicles 33:3, 5; Nehemiah 9:6; Jeremiah 7:18; 8:2; 19:13; Hosea 13:4; and Zephaniah 1:5.[7] Note the following five observations about these passages in the context of the rest of the Scriptures.

1. All nine of these uses of *stratia* are linked with the Greek word *ouranos*, which means "heaven." In other words, in the Septuagint, *stratia* is a word used either for an earthly army (nineteen times) or a heavenly army (nine times). Note that Luke 2:13 falls in line, of course, with the second of these uses, "heavenly host."

2. All but one of these occurrences of *stratia* translate the specific Hebrew word that occurs in the KJV, RSV, and NRSV as "the LORD of *hosts*." The one that doesn't fit this pattern is Jeremiah 7:18, which has some unique translation problems.[8]

3. It is possible that at least some of the remaining eight occurrences of *stratia* refer to the stars as created by God. For example, when Hosea 13:4 talks about the Lord God who created the heavens and the earth and all the *stratia* of heaven, he may indeed be referring to those physical bodies in the sky—sun, moon, and stars (see also Jer. 8:2).[9]

4. In a sense, however, the question of whether the *stratia* of heaven in these eight passages denotes physical objects in the heavens or spiritual beings is a moot one, since in the ancient world these two were closely related. To the pagan nations around Israel, the major heavenly bodies were gods whom they worshiped. The Egyptians worshiped the sun god, who went by various names, such as Atum, Re, Amun, and Amun-Re. In Mesopotamia, Shamash was the sun god (closely related to the Hebrew word for sun, *shemesh*), Sin was the moon god, and Ishtar a star goddess associated with the planet Venus. These were all deities linked with heavenly bodies, deserving of worship by the heathen nations. Note this comment in *The Dictionary of Biblical Imagery*:

The "heavenly hosts" made famous by English translations of the Bible have two distinct meanings: one is a
reference to the stars; the other to God's celestial armies,
presumably of angels. Sometimes the two references
seem to merge. In fact, the two meanings of the Hebrew
phrase for "host of heaven" . . . namely, "celestial bodies" and "angelic hosts," reflect a probable association
between angels and stars and planets in the Hebrew
imagination. The heavenly hosts of stars, moreover,
sometimes have associations of idolatry, since surrounding pagan nations were given to astrology and worship of
the heavenly bodies.[10]

Not only the heathen nations worshiped the sun, moon,
and stars of heaven. The voice of the biblical prophets de-
clares that the Israelites also adopted these gods as worthy
of worship. Manasseh, for example, set up sacred groves
and cultic pillars and bowed down to worship and serve
"all the *stratia* of heaven" (2 Chron. 33:3, 5)—that is, all the
starry hosts. These were not simply physical objects in the
sky; they were gods, they were spiritual beings.

5. In at least two of these references (1 Kings 22:19; Neh.
9:6), the *stratia* of heaven refers to created spiritual beings
who are on the Lord's side, not false gods. Another term
for these would be "angels who serve the LORD." Presumably they refer to spiritual beings, angels, who formed the
armies of the Lord. In any case, in this expression the military connotations are clear.

An interesting story appears in the Old Testament. Although
the term *stratia* is not used in this instance in the Septuagint, I

believe it nevertheless illustrates the work of this spiritual army of God. In 2 Kings 6, Elisha, through divine revelation, had been tipping off the king of Israel as to where the enemy Arameans were going to strike next. The king of Aram suspected a spy in their ranks, but one of his officers informed him about the revelations of Elisha. The king of Aram ordered his soldiers to capture Elisha and sent a strong force of horses and chariots to surround the town of Dothan, where he was living. Elisha's servant was terrified, but Elisha prayed that the servant's eyes might be opened. When they were opened, the servant "looked and saw the hills full of horses and chariots of fire all around Elisha" (v. 17). These were the armies of the Lord, ready to do his bidding on behalf of his servants.

Moreover, in another significant story in the Old Testament, the heavenly hosts/armies of the Lord are clearly related to the stars. Note these two parallel lines from the song of Deborah in Judges 5:20: "from the heavens the stars fought, from their courses they fought against Sisera." These "stars" of heaven are those spiritual beings who had fought for God's people and against Sisera and his soldiers to defeat them.

How does this military imagery, then, intersect with the Christmas story? In chapter 2 we discussed the evidence in the Bible that Christmas was the beginning of a celestial war. Jesus came to destroy the works of the Devil, and Satan reciprocated by trying to destroy Jesus. That overall theme intersects now with the "multitude of the heavenly host" (NRSV), who appear to the shepherds in the fields of Bethlehem.

We can look at this issue as follows: Throughout Jesus' life and ministry, he had numerous encounters with demons, the cohorts of Satan. The encounter that receives the most extended discussion is the one recorded in Mark 5:1–20 (cf. also Matt. 8:28–34; Luke 8:26–39). The demon who inhabited a man living among the tombs in the regions of the Gerasenes accosted Jesus by recognizing his name: "Jesus, Son of the Most High God" (v. 7). When Jesus in turn asked the demon his name, he gave it as "Legion . . . for we are many" (v. 9). *Legion* is a military term for a division of six thousand soldiers in the Roman army. This man was actually inhabited by an army of demons, which suggests that all of the encounters that Jesus had with demon possession were encounters with spiritual soldiers of wickedness.

Toward the end of Jesus' life, when, as I suggested in chapter 2, Satan attempted to destroy Jesus for the seventh and last time in the garden of Gethsemane, Jesus said something remarkable. He likely said it to Peter, who, as we know from John 18:10, struck the servant of the high priest with his sword, cutting off the servant's ear. Our Savior openly admitted that he had always had a spiritual army at his disposal: "Do you think I cannot call on my Father, and he will at once put at my disposal more than twelve legions of angels?" (Matt. 26:53).

It is significant, too, that Matthew 26:53; Mark 5:9; Luke 8:30 are the only occurrences of the word *legion* in the Greek New Testament. Satan had his legions, and Jesus had his legions. They had been at war with each other throughout the entire ministry of Jesus. During the time Jesus was on the earth, there was a war going on in the spiritual realm, unseen by human beings, between the heavenly soldiers of Jesus and those of the Devil. It seems to me that those legions of angels who were ready to do the bidding of Jesus in Matthew 26 are identical to the multitude of the heavenly host, the *stratia*, that is out on the fields of Bethlehem.

In other words, the song that these heavenly angels sing, which we will examine in the next chapter, is not sung first and foremost by a heavenly choir, though I don't doubt for a minute that they were trained in music as well as in military procedures. It is sung by legions of heavenly soldiers whose Commander in Chief has just been born, and they know that full-fledged war is just ahead of them. And they are standing ready to do his bidding, probably armed in full battle regalia. The song sung to the shepherds, then, is essentially the celestial version of "Hail to the Chief." Christmas is the beginning of war.

## CHAPTER 9

# The Song of the Angels

Glory to God in the highest, and on earth peace, good will toward men.

(Luke 2:14 KJV)

You see these words on hundreds of Christmas cards during the Christmas season. In churches, on streets, and hanging from store ceilings, large banners shout out, "Peace on earth" or "Good will toward men." It is probably this version of the song of the angels in Luke 2:14 that has, in fact, largely been responsible for the temporary cease-fires that I referred to in the preface to this book. This song suggests that Christmas is a time when peace descends on earth because of the birth of the Prince of Peace. So, to honor him, we declare December 25 as a day to stop fighting.

So how can there be anything to this song that intersects with a dark side of Christmas? There are two facets about this song that we need to explore.

The first relates to whether this song expresses a fact or should be read as a prayer. You see, there is no verb in this song—not in the Greek and not even in the English. So just by looking at the song, you cannot tell which of two understandings of the song the heavenly army is singing: "Now that the Savior, Christ the Lord, has been born, peace exists on earth," or, "Now that the Savior, Christ the Lord, has been born, we pray that peace will eventually descend upon earth." In other words, is this song an assertion or is it a prayer? To put it in terms of Greek grammar, is the form of the verb *to be* that we could apply to this clause an indicative or an optative?

Based on what we saw in the previous chapter, where the heavenly army is fully aware that war is ahead, it seems that this song is a prayer, not an assertion of fact. Is this an arbitrary choice? Did I choose it because it fits with the theme of this book?

Neither. This song has the same flavor as what the writers of the New Testament letters use as a salutation or in ending them with a benediction. Almost all the New Testament letters begin with some version of "Grace and peace to you from God our Father and from the Lord Jesus Christ" (Rom. 1:7). And many of the letters, especially those written by Paul, end with some version of "May the grace of the Lord Jesus Christ, and the love of God, and the fellowship of the Holy Spirit be with you all" (2 Cor. 13:14). These salutations and benedictions also do not usually have a Greek verb included. And like the song of the heavenly army, these verbless phrases could possibly be read either as assertions or as prayers.

But there are three opening greetings in the Greek New Testament where an actual Greek verb is included, and in all three cases the verb form is identical: "Grace and peace be multiplied to you in the knowledge of God and of Jesus our Lord" (2 Peter 1:2 NASB; see also 1 Peter 1:2; Jude 2). The actual verb form is *plethyneie*, and it is the optative form, technically called an optative of wish.

In other words, the writers of these letters are praying that God will multiply his grace and peace to his people as we grow in our knowledge of him and of his Son, Jesus Christ.

This, I believe, is what the angel soldiers are singing on the fields of Bethlehem. They are praying that since the Savior has been born, since God has sent his Son, all glory may be given to God, who has given this stupendous gift, and they are praying that peace may now descend upon earth. But being a heavenly army of legions of angels and knowing who the enemy is, they are fully aware that this peace will not come easily. They must fight many battles against the Devil and his legions, and the final establishment of that kingdom of peace still lies in the future.

Those battles are still going on today and peace still eludes us, though we are certain that Christ will win the eventual victory. According to the vision that God gave John in Revelation 12, while there is no longer war in heaven, the Devil has been cast to this earth, where he now wages "war against the rest of her [the woman's] offspring [i.e., the church]—those who obey God's commandments and hold to the testimony of Jesus" (v. 17 NIV). The apostle Paul also recognizes that we as God's people are in the midst of an ongoing struggle, "not against flesh and blood, but against the rulers, against the authorities, against the powers of this dark world and against the spiritual forces of evil in the heavenly realms" (Eph. 6:12). That is why we are given spiritual armor (vv. 13–17). There is not peace on earth yet; that will only come when the Devil and "death and Hades [are] thrown into the lake of fire . . . [which is] the second death" (Rev. 20:14).

The second facet in the song of the heavenly army that needs discussion is a peculiar element in the most common version of this song, "on earth peace, good will toward men." This is the way the song reads in the King James Version, but you will not see it translated that way in any modern version of the Bible except for the New King James Version. The NIV, for example, reads, "on earth, peace to men on whom his favor rests," and the NRSV reads, "on earth peace among those whom he favors!" (Rarely, by the way, do you see these translations on Christmas cards and holiday banners.)

What's going on here? The difference between these two translations rests on a single Greek letter that was dropped from the word for "good will." From the time that the New Testament was written to the time that the printing press was invented, the Bible was copied by hand. There are more than five thousand handwritten manuscripts of all or parts of the New Testament, and as one might expect, these copies are not all identical. In fact, there are thousands and thousands of what are called "variant readings," none of which, however, changes the overall teaching of the New Testament. Scholars use various techniques in attempting to determine which of the variants was the original version, and scholars are pretty well in agreement that the Greek version that underlies the King James translation of Luke 2:14 was not what Luke actually wrote.

I said above that the difference between the King James Version and modern translations of the words *good will* is a single letter. The Greek word for "good will" is *eudokia*. This is the way the word appears in the Greek version that the translators of the King James Version used, and it is parallel to the word for "peace" (*eirene*). Virtually all scholars agree, however, that Luke wrote *eudokias*, which translates to "of good will," because this is what the oldest and best manuscripts of the New Testament have.[1] That means, then, that a fairly word-for-word translation of the Greek of Luke 2:14 goes like this: "and on earth peace to men of good will."

The question then, is this: What does "men of good will" (or better, "people of good will," since the word *anthropois* includes both male and female) mean? Whose "good will" is being referred to? Almost every scholar recognizes that this use of *eudokia* bears similarity to what Paul wrote about in Ephesians 1:5, 9: "He predestined us to be adopted as his sons through Jesus Christ, in accordance with his *pleasure* [*eudokia*] and will . . . he made known to us the mystery of his will according to his *good pleasure* [*eudokia*]" (NIV). In fact, in Luke's only other use of the word *eudokia*, he relates it unmistakably to God's "good pleasure": "I praise you, Father, Lord of heaven and earth, because you have hidden these things from the wise and learned, and revealed them to little children. Yes, Father, for this was your good pleasure [*eudokia*]" (Luke 10:21).

In other words, the prayer song of the heavenly army in Luke 2:14 is a prayer that those on whom God's favor rests (that is, his chosen people) may experience an incredible peace on this earth through our Savior, Christ the Lord. The primary focus of the prayer for peace that the angelic army sings about is not a generic prayer that all nations on earth may experience peace in their international relationships. Rather, it is that God's people may experience peace, *shalom* (to use the Hebrew word), within their hearts—in their relationship with God, in their relationships with other human beings, and in relationship to themselves. This song is virtually identical, therefore, to the opening salutations and closing benedictions of the New Testament letters: "Grace and *peace* to you from God our Father and from the Lord Jesus Christ."

Probably the reason why we have almost invariably related "the Christmas peace" to international relationships is that we, in general, define "peace" as the absence of war. If two countries are not fighting each other in some fashion, even if it be a "cold war," there is a measure of peace between them. But the definition of "peace" in the Bible is a much richer concept than the absence of something. Both the word *shalom* in the Old Testament and the word *eirene* in the New Testament have, at their core, the idea of harmony and wholeness. *Shalom* is a word that "denotes personal well-being, prosperity, or bodily health." Moreover, it "means more than simply the absence of war, for it also speaks of completeness, wholeness, and harmony."² Similar things can be said about the Greek word *eirene*.

And for the Christian, such harmony and unity is only possible through Jesus Christ, the "Prince of Peace." The apostle Paul summarizes this comprehensive message of peace through Jesus in Ephesians 2:14–15, where he emphasizes how all artificial human barriers, such as that between Jew and Gentile, find their unity in Christ: "For he himself [Jesus Christ] is our peace, who has made the two one and has destroyed the barrier, the dividing wall of hostility, by abolishing in his flesh the law with its commandments and regulations. His purpose was to create in himself one new man out of the two [Jew and Gentile], thus making peace" (NIV). And the angels in Bethlehem are praying, through their song, that this peace may indeed descend on and be lived out through those who have a personal relationship with Jesus Christ.

Now admittedly this peace is not a negative element in the Christmas story. This is a glorious message. But it is important to see the true message of the song of the heavenly army so that we do not think that its essence is the imposition of an artificial international peace among the nations. While there is certainly nothing wrong with a temporary cease-fire at Christmastime— would that there might never be wars and rumors of wars among the nations!—this is not the peace that the angels sang about. It is, rather, "since we have been justified through faith, we have peace with God through our Lord Jesus Christ" (Rom. 5:1), and through peace with him we can have, and should work toward, peace in our homes and peace in our churches and peace within ourselves.

## CHAPTER 10

# The Words of Simeon

You've probably noticed that in my probing of the not-so-silent night of Christmas, I'm going through the traditional passages in the Bible that deal with the birth of Jesus in somewhat chronological order. So from the story of the birth of Jesus and the message given to the shepherds on the fields of Bethlehem, I am now moving to the story of what is called the presentation of Jesus in the temple (Luke 2:22–38). This is not generally considered part of the Christmas story, but it is certainly part of the nativity and infancy of Jesus.

Here is why. No one questions that the visit of the magi to Bethlehem is a part of the Christmas story, but that visit chronologically must have taken place after Luke 2:22–38. As we know from that story, immediately after the visit of the magi, Joseph and Mary had to flee to Egypt, so the presentation of Jesus in the temple in Jerusalem must have occurred before the magi arrived in Bethlehem. Moreover, according to Matthew 2 (which we will look at in our final chapter), the magi did not come to a manger but "to the house" where the child was (see Matt. 2:11). Furthermore, Jesus may have actually been a toddler by this time. Recall that King Herod determined which babies in Bethlehem to kill "in accordance with the time he had learned from the Magi" about the appearance of the star, which had announced the birth of the king of the Jews (Matt. 2:16). Apparently that star appeared up to two years prior to their visit.

In other words, if the visit of the magi is a legitimate passage for sermons on the infant Jesus, a look at Luke's story of Jesus' presentation in the temple is equally legitimate to examine. And there is, indeed, in this story plenty that reminds us of the incredible sadness and pain linked with the Christmas story.

Forty days after the birth of a son, the Jewish law required a woman to go to the temple to offer sacrifices for her purification. If she could not afford a lamb and a pigeon or dove, then two birds would suffice (Lev. 12:2–8). Joseph and Mary fell into this latter category.[1] Their poverty, in fact, recalls one of the elements discussed in chapter 7 on the humiliation of Jesus' birth and childhood.

While Joseph and Mary are there in the temple, an old man named Simeon arrives, having been prompted by the Spirit. The Holy Spirit had revealed to him that he would not die until "he had seen the Lord's Christ" (Luke 2:26 NIV). This was the moment! He takes the child into his arms and sings a song that is now called the *Nunc Dimittis*. We might expect him to sing a song of thanksgiving to God for giving his Messiah to the world. Instead, he sings a song that indicates he is now ready to die because his eyes have seen God's prepared salvation (lit.): "Now dismiss [in Latin: *nunc dimittis*] your servant, Lord, according to your word in peace" (v. 29).

Once again, as we have seen so often in these chapters, death is in the air. True, Simeon does not betray sadness in his own approaching death, for God has fulfilled a promise to him. But human death is never an inherently happy event. It is always a reminder of the sin of Adam and its disastrous results for the human race.

But Simeon's subsequent words after the song are even sadder and heavier. For he speaks these words to Mary, the mother of Jesus: "This child is destined to cause the falling and rising of many in Israel, and to be a sign that will be spoken against, so that the thoughts of many hearts will be revealed. And a sword will pierce your own soul too" (vv. 34–35). Simeon is here charting what will be the course of Jesus' life. Three dark elements stand out in the song.

First, as Jesus enters his public ministry, says Simeon, many will fall because of him. That is, he will be a stumbling block to many of the Jews—those who refuse to believe in him. Yes, it is true that there will be those who believe in him and who will rise to a new life in Christ. But as far as Simeon's speech is concerned, the falling of "many in Israel" is the more dominant reality; it stands first in his words.

This is the theme that burdens the apostle Paul so terribly in Romans 9–11, where he struggles with the reality that so many of his fellow Jews are refusing to acknowledge Jesus as the Messiah. It burdens him so much that he writes, "I have great sorrow and unceasing anguish in my heart. For I could wish that I myself were cursed and cut off from Christ for the sake of my brothers, those of my own race, the people of Israel" (9:2–4 NIV).

A few verses later in Romans 9:32–33, Paul states specifically that the majority of Israel "stumbled over the 'stumbling stone.' As it is written: 'See, I lay in Zion a stone that causes men to stumble and a rock that makes them fall'" (NIV; see also 1 Cor. 1:23). As the apostle later acknowledges, during his lifetime only a remnant are being saved (Rom. 11:5; cf. 9:27). This is a heavy burden for the apostle to bear, and Simeon acknowledges this sad reality already in his comments to Mary.

Second, Jesus is "a sign that will be spoken against." This phrase obviously ties in closely with the overall rejection of Jesus by the Jews. But it testifies to more than that. It refers to an *active rejection* of the message of Jesus. Mary has, we've already argued, experienced such rejection herself both in Nazareth and in Bethlehem on the part of her and Joseph's relatives. But rejection of Jesus will not be limited to just these close relatives. There will be an active rejection of Jesus on the part of the Jewish leadership. In our final chapter we will see this clearly in the story of the visit of the magi. That rejection will increase throughout Jesus' ministry until it culminates in his crucifixion, instigated by the Jewish ruling council, the Sanhedrin (see John 11:45–53). Thus, the shadow of the cross hangs over the presentation of Jesus in the temple.

Third, the final element in Simeon's words to Mary that forebodes darkness is a personal address to Mary herself: "And a sword will pierce your own soul too." A sword has, of course, already pierced her soul, but the sadness she has experienced the previous few months will pale in significance to what will take place in a number of stories in the Gospels after Jesus started his ministry.

Mary's "pierced soul" begins at the wedding in Cana of Galilee recorded in John 2:1–11. After the bridegroom runs out of wine, Mary comes to Jesus with the message, "They have no more wine" (v. 3). And Jesus replies, "Dear woman, why do you involve me? . . . My time has not yet come" (v. 4 NIV). Admittedly, for anyone to address a married woman as "woman" ("dear" has been added in the NIV) was not a sign of disrespect in the first century. But note that Jesus does not acknowledge that this is his mother whom he is addressing. Through his words Jesus is beginning to distance himself from his mother. I suspect a twinge of pain goes through Mary's soul at this point.

The next incident chronologically for additional pain in Mary's heart most likely occurs when Jesus preached at Nazareth, the town where he grew up and the place where Mary still lived with the rest of her family. Jesus receives an opportunity to speak in the synagogue on the Sabbath, and he accepts the opportunity (Luke 4:16–30). At first the people of Nazareth are impressed by what Jesus says, but then he switches gears in his message and begins to talk about evidences in the Old Testament of God's love for non-Jewish people. By the end of his sermon, the townsfolk are so angry that they take him "to the brow of the hill on which the town was built, in order to throw him off the cliff" (v. 29). Jesus eludes them at this point and "walked right through the crowd," untouched. But I wonder what went through the heart of Mary as she saw other people in Nazareth, including some of her relatives, grab her son with the intent of killing him. The sword went into her soul just a little bit deeper.

The next story is told in Mark 3:31–35. The family of Jesus—presumably Mary with her other children—is coming to see him, perhaps even to get him to tone down his ministry because, "they said, 'He is out of his mind'" (v. 21). When the message reaches Jesus that "your mother and brothers are outside looking for you," Jesus replies, "'Who are my mother and my brothers?' . . . Then he looked at those seated in a circle around him and said, 'Here are my mother and my brothers! Whoever does God's will is my brother and sister and mother'" (vv. 33–35).

These words drive the sword into Mary's soul a tad deeper still. Jesus is here actually refusing to name Mary as his mother. Instead, he insists, he now has a new family—those people seated around him who are doing the will of God. Imagine Mary's feelings as the word comes back to her, "Jesus is refusing to see you!

He doesn't even acknowledge you as his mother." Why does Jesus refuse to see his family? We don't really know. Was it perhaps because Jesus' "own brothers did not believe in him" (John 7:5)? If so, Mary is then caught between what she knows about Jesus—that he is not just her son but the Son of God, the Messiah—and what her other children think about him. How terribly conflicting this must have been for her. And since almost all scholars agree that by this time Joseph has most likely died, she does not have him to lean on and to help make her other children toe the line about who their oldest brother is.

The final story in his distancing of himself from Mary occurs in John 19:16–27 when Jesus is hanging on the cross. According to the gospel of John, Mary is there at the foot of the cross, witnessing the horrible treatment that Jesus has been receiving (v. 25). One can only imagine the sword that must have been stabbing her heart at this horrendous moment. And then Jesus speaks to her. One might expect Jesus to address his mother with words such as, "Mother, I am so sorry you have to see this. But it's going to be okay. After three days I am going to rise, and you will see me alive again."

But those are not the words recorded by John. Rather, this is what we read: "When Jesus saw his mother there, and the disciple whom he loved standing nearby, he said to his mother, 'Dear woman, here is your son,' and to the disciple, 'Here is your mother'" (vv. 26–27 NIV). The sword just plunged deeper still. Not only does Jesus for the last time refuse to call Mary his mother, but he actually says to this effect, "Woman, you are no longer to consider me your son; rather, consider John (the beloved disciple) as your substitute son." And then to John he says, "Take good care of this woman as you would your own mother." Jesus has totally distanced himself now from Mary as his mother, and for the woman who bore him, that must have hurt deeply.

Just to qualify this part of the story, I do think it is clear why Jesus had to gradually distance himself from his earthly relationship to Mary as his mother, though Mary may not have realized it at the time. Jesus knew that the only way for anyone to become a child of God was to believe in him. No one can earn his or her way into his heavenly kingdom. That means that not even Mary will be able to stand before God on the day of judgment and say, "Of course I deserve eternal life. After all, Jesus is *my son!* Look at all that I went through for him!" Even Mary can only receive a room prepared for her in the Father's house if she releases her hold on Jesus as her son and instead believes in him as her Savior and receives him in her pierced heart as her Lord.

As difficult as it may have been for Jesus, he wants to make sure that Mary commits her life to him. And thanks be to God that she does, for she, along with her other children, are there in the upper room (Acts 1:13–14), waiting the ten days between Jesus' ascension into heaven and Pentecost, when they receive his outpouring of God's Spirit.

But this does not mean that the gradual distancing of Jesus from Mary, his mother, was easy on her. In fact, it was downright painful. As Simeon prophesied to Mary when the baby Jesus was forty days old, "a sword will pierce your own soul too." Simeon was charting out here what the life of Mary would be during the time of Jesus' ministry, and it would be as if someone was stabbing her in the heart. This is the heart-wrenching pathway that God had planned for the mother of our Savior in order that she might attain eternal life with her son, God's Son.

## CHAPTER 11

# The Visit of
# the Magi

As I mentioned in the opening comments to the previous chapter, the visit of the magi to see the Christ child is the last of the events chronologically that we traditionally associate with Christmas. Most Christmas pageants show the magi visiting the Babe in the manger, usually along with the shepherds, but this depiction is called "telescoping"—events that were in reality separated in time but are placed together for the sake of drama and narrative.

Of all the events in the Christmas story, the record of the visit of the magi contains probably the greatest number of obviously sad and painful elements. Some of these we have already looked at. In chapter 1, we noted that one of the gifts the magi presented to the Christ child was "myrrh," a noun that occurs elsewhere in the New Testament only in connection with the burial of Christ. And a verb related to this noun is used in the crucifixion story with reference to a pain reliever that Jesus was given while on the cross, when he was experiencing excruciating pain. In other words, already as a young child, though perhaps Joseph and Mary do not know it, Jesus' death and burial are looming on the horizon.

Another dark element of the story of the magi, one that we looked at in chapter 2, was the aftermath of their visit. After the magi had left to return to the East, using a route that did not take them back to the palace of King Herod, he became angry and ordered all the baby boys of Bethlehem, two years old and younger, to be ruthlessly slaughtered. With these age parameters he hoped to make sure that "the king of the Jews" would be included among the slaughter. Only God's intervention through a dream to Joseph enabled Jesus to escape the sword of the earthly king.

But there is more in the story of the magi that needs to be told. The magi were most likely astrologers from the area of Persia. For centuries people from this area had been famous for their knowledge of the movement of the stars and the planets. One night the magi discovered something in the sky that they had never seen before—a new star. I will not speculate on what it may have been (a nova, a convergence of planets, or a comet are some of the suggestions). They began to examine all the writings available to them to see if they could discover what this celestial phenomenon meant. It would appear as if they had a copy of the Hebrew Pentateuch in their possession, for Numbers 24:17 (NIV) reads,

> I see him, but not now;
>     I behold him, but not near.
> A star will come out of Jacob;
>     a scepter will rise out of Israel.
> He will crush the foreheads of Moab,
>     the skulls of all the sons of Sheth.

We have no verification in the text that this passage came to their attention as a result of their research, though it is a reasonable assumption, since the verse talks about someone who will bear a scepter—hence, a king—and whose coming is associated with a special star. In any case, what is certain is that the magi concluded that the "star" they had seen "in the east" was linked with the birth of the "king of the Jews" (Matt. 2:2 NIV). So they traveled hundreds of miles to Jerusalem, where apparently King Herod was temporarily staying, perhaps at the time of one of the Jewish feasts. The magi sought an audience with Herod in order to ask the question, "Where is the one who has been born king of the Jews?"

The magi, of course, assumed the child would be a son of the present king, Herod. But they were wrong. It had been a long time since Herod had been the father of a child. Neither did the magi know the tyrannical jealousy and the paranoid personality of Herod, who had recently killed his favorite wife and two of his sons (and later a third one) because he was suspicious that they might try to dethrone him. Nevertheless, Herod played it cool with the magi, even though their news "disturbed" him (v. 3). He decided to ask the Jewish chief priests and scribes to tell him where the expected king of the Jews would be born.

Herod apparently knew enough of Jewish hopes and aspirations that they were looking forward to a coming Son of David, a coming king, a Messiah. Just like Anna (see Luke 2:36–38), all of the Jews were "looking forward to the redemption of Jerusalem" (v. 38). Like Simeon, God's people were looking ahead to the arrival of "the consolation of Israel" (v. 25). The entire Hebrew Scriptures contained prophecies that foretold various aspects of the coming Messiah, particularly the promise that he would sit on David's throne and restore David's kingdom. This had been their hope for hundreds of years!

One would think, then, that when the magi came with their knowledge that the coming Son of David, the Messiah, had been born, the Jews in Jerusalem would rejoice with exceedingly great joy. But what do we read? Not only was Herod "frightened" at the message of the magi, but so also was "all Jerusalem with him" (Matt. 2:3 NRSV). Rather than rejoice at the word the magi brought about the birth of "the king of the Jews," all the Jews in Jerusalem were quaking in fear.

Now I suppose their fear was well founded. They knew Herod's personality, especially the paranoia of his declining years. They knew he was unpredictable and that Jerusalem could end up in a bloodbath if Herod's ire became stirred. But the fact that everyone became terribly afraid and no one seemed excited or hopeful is indeed sad. Here the Jewish people are being informed that their Messiah has been born, the fulfillment of the hope that had sustained them as a people for generation after generation, and they are now cringing in fear, terrified even to acknowledge that possibility.

There are in the Old Testament stories of several Jewish men who took God at his word and who refused to bow to the eccentricities of a pagan king. And they did so fearlessly, even though it placed their lives in danger. Three of them were thrown into a fiery furnace (Dan. 3), and the fourth one (Daniel) was thrown into a den of hungry lions (Dan. 6). But the Lord protected the lives of all four of them. Yet at the arrival of the magi, no one in Jerusalem seems to have reflected on these stories or decided, in spite of the fear of the king, either to celebrate the birth of the king of the Jews or even to accompany the magi to Bethlehem.

In fact, the story gets worse. Herod summons the chief priests and the scribes and asks them in which town the Messiah, the Christ, the promised king, would be born, according to the teachings of their Hebrew Scriptures. The response of the Jewish leaders is about as nonchalant as one can get. They simply quote for Herod the prophecy of Micah 5:2, that the Messiah will be born in the little town of Bethlehem, as if they are answering a *Jeopardy* question. Because they do not need to ask for a day to research the question, one gets the sense they are quick to answer and then get out of Herod's presence, lest they come face to face with his wrath.

This is sad indeed. In chapters 4 and 6 of this book I asserted that Jesus was rejected by his own family—perhaps even by Mary's own mother and father. And the extended Davidic family in Bethlehem appears to have snubbed Joseph and Mary when they showed up at the *katalyma*, where they hoped to find lodging and perhaps assistance with the birth, should the baby Mary was carrying be born that evening. The Old Testament passage I quoted there is relevant here as well: "He was despised and rejected by men" (Isa. 53:3 NIV). And so is John 1:11: "He came to that which was his own, but his own did not receive him."

In those earlier chapters, I cited the above passages as applying to the family circles related to Jesus. But it was not only they who rejected him, but the entire Jewish nation, especially their leadership. "All Jerusalem," who could not have avoided seeing these strangers from Persia enter their city, was deeply disturbed and frightened at the message the magi brought about the king of the Jews and wanted nothing further to do with it. And if that was not enough, the Jewish leaders were willing to give Herod the information he wanted about where the Messiah would be born, knowing full well how he would react. And then in fright they high-tailed it out of his presence. In a real sense, they were informing Herod where he could go to kill their Messiah.

In other words, the New Testament suggests that Jesus was despised and rejected by all of God's people. The only probable exceptions were Zechariah and Elizabeth and the lowly shepherds

on the fields of Bethlehem, who "returned [to their sheep], glorify-
ing and praising God for all the things they had heard and seen"
(Luke 2:20). No one else among God's people who had been informed about the birth of the promised Messiah was eager to see
that baby when the time of his birth came, or even to acknowledge
that it was happening. This is indeed tragic.

# Conclusion

P lease don't get me wrong. I love Christmas. I love to sing Christmas carols. I love the brightly decorated trees. I love the festivities. I even love to preach on the Christmas story. I love many of the things we associate with the Christmas season.

But I do not think we do the Bible justice when the only thing we see in the Christmas story is the joy and the excitement, when all we reflect on is the thrilling fact that a special baby, God's one and only Son, has been born. We need to see the whole story, with all of its ugliness, all of its darkness, all of its sadness. Our celebration of Christmas will never be complete until we do.

In what practical ways might the biblical picture presented in this book shape our celebration of the nativity of Jesus? The most obvious thing, of course, is to resist as much as possible the commercialism of Christmas. Christmas offers a special time to reflect on our lives as sinful human beings and our need for a redeemer, the one who died on the cross for us. The purpose of this season is not to see how much we can add to the coffers of malls and discount stores. A "good Christmas" is not defined by whether sales this year have surpassed last year, but by how well we have entered into the spirit of how the Bible describes those events that happened in the Holy Land more than two thousand years ago.

Any conscientious Christian parent uses words, of course, to teach their children the importance of the true meaning of Christmas. But it wouldn't hurt parents to use examples as well to reflect the deeper implications inherent in the birth of our Savior. Let's consider making a concerted effort to simplify our celebration of Christmas. Several books are available on this idea. Perhaps you can decide that there will be only one gift per family member under the tree, if you even choose to use a tree. Give the money you might have spent on additional gifts to organizations that are trying to help needy people with the basics of human life, such as clean and safe water, sufficient food, and sustainable income that can be generated from sewing machines and livestock.

It wouldn't hurt either to have a cross standing next to the nativity scene, to remind us that this baby Jesus was destined to die on the cross. Put ornaments on the tree to reflect Good Friday—make them by hand, if need be. One of the favorite ornaments I purchased many years ago was a glass ball painted black with the words "O sacred head, now wounded" printed on it. It was always one of the first ornaments I put on the tree until our cat knocked down the tree one year and that ornament broke. My daughter, though, made a replacement for me.

Pastors can do wonders by using the Advent season to set the tone for Christmas. When I was a full-time pastor, I was constantly looking for some new slant that I could use to preach during the Advent/Christmas season, and I think a series of messages on the not-so-silent night of Christmas would give your parishioners much to think about as they head toward December 25. If your church has a cross prominently displayed, don't hesitate to draw attention to the connection between the crèche and the cross. Or perhaps even design a cross and interior lighting so that a dark shadow is cast over a nativity scene. Your congregation will not forget that picture.

Remember too that there are many who for any number of reasons may be going through a time of pain—a death in the family, an empty place at the holiday table, conflict in the home, divorce, serious illness, even loved ones involved in a war somewhere. Emphasize that such people can find in Joseph and Mary kindred spirits who understand them in their trials and hurts. All too often, I fear, we as pastors present the picture from the pulpit that if people are not feeling the brightness and joy of this season, they are not entering the true spirit of Christmas.

I really don't know what to do about the majestic Christmas pageants that have become traditional in some churches. Just once I'd like to see a pageant in which the relatives of Joseph and Mary flagrantly refuse their guest room to that heart-broken couple and relegate them instead to the barn. I would like to see a manger scene without the magi filling the stage with pomp and expensive presents. I would like to see tears in the eyes of Joseph and Mary and fear in their hearts as they reflect on what the future might hold. I doubt if such pageants have been written, and even if they were, they probably wouldn't sell. It doesn't fit our Christmas mythology.

As I reflect on the Christmas stories in the Bible, a darkness fills my own soul, just as darkness fills my soul when I read about Good Friday. A few years ago, I was teaching the Gospels to some young pastors in Trinidad, trying to get across to them what was really happening to Mary and Joseph. I found I could hardly finish the lesson because tears began to fill my eyes as I thought of the pain of that young, unmarried couple. Yet at the same time my heart was filled with gratitude, because Jesus—along with his parents—was willing to go through all of this pain and rejection so that I might receive forgiveness and the gift of eternal life.

I am convinced that if we spend any amount of time personally reflecting on this not-so-silent night of Christmas, we will not be as eager to participate in the traditional things we associate with the season. Rather, we will want to spend our time in quiet meditation and in grateful devotion for God's incredible gift to us. "Today in the town of David a Savior has been born to you; he is Christ the Lord. This will be a sign to you: You will find a baby wrapped in cloths and lying in a manger" (Luke 2:11–12 NIV).

*Gloria in excelsis Deo.*
*Soli Deo gloria.*

# Notes

## INTRODUCTION
1. Accounts of the event are widely available on the Internet; for example, see http://www.firstworldwar.com/features/christmas truce.htm.

## CHAPTER 1: BORN TO DIE
1. The firstborn male human being was also claimed by the Lord, but he could be redeemed for a set redemption price and thus escape the sacrifice (Num. 18:15–16).

## CHAPTER 2: THE BEGINNING OF WAR
1. See David W. Baker, "Isaiah, Jeremiah, Lamentations, Ezekiel, Daniel," vol. 4 of *Zondervan Illustrated Bible Backgrounds Commentary: Old Testament*, ed. John H. Walton (Grand Rapids: Zondervan, 2009), comment on Isaiah 30:7.
2. See John W. Hilber, "Psalms," vol. 5 of *Zondervan Illustrated Bible Backgrounds Commentary: Old Testament*, ed. John H. Walton (Grand Rapids: Zondervan, 2009), comment on Psalm 89:9–10.

3. Much of this material on Satan's attempts on the life of Jesus is taken from my article, "The Heavenly Army on the Fields of Bethlehem," *Calvin Theological Journal* 43 (2008): 301–11.

4. First Corinthians 2:8 states that "none of the rulers of this age understood it [God's secret wisdom about the power of the cross], for if they had, they would not have crucified the Lord of glory." If the "rulers of this age [*aion*]" refers to malevolent spiritual hosts, that would suggest, of course, that Satan was unaware of the significance of Jesus' dying *on a cross*. For a number of reasons, however, I believe that Paul is referring primarily here to human rulers, not the "rulers . . . authorities . . . powers . . . [and] spiritual forces of evil in the heavenly realms" referred to in Ephesians 6:12, and certainly not Satan, their prince. Cf. Verlyn D. Verbrugge, "1 Corinthians," *Expositor's Bible Commentary: Revised Edition*, ed. Tremper Longman III and David E. Garland (Grand Rapids: Zondervan, 2008), 11:177.

## CHAPTER 4: MARY'S SHAME

1. See Matthew J. Marohl, *Joseph's Dilemma: "Honor Killing" in the Birth Narrative of Matthew* (Eugene, OR: Wipf and Stock, 2008).

2. Ibid., 1–20.

3. Ibid., 38–54.

4. While the 2006 movie *The Nativity Story* contains many historical inaccuracies, it is correct to this extent, that because Mary had become pregnant prior to wedlock, according to the Old Testament law she could legally be stoned (Deut. 22:20–22).

5. I do admit there is a long tradition that links Joseph's registering with the phrase "with Mary," since when the New Testament was divided up into verses in the 1550s, Luke 2:5 begins with the Greek infinitive "to register," and it is followed immediately

by "with Mary." But I know of no ancient tradition that required husbands and wives—and certainly not those pledged to be married—to register together. Joseph was traveling with Mary, not registering with Mary.

6. For those who know Greek, here are the technical details. The phrase translated "the one pledged to be married" is a participle; it is preceded by the definite article, which makes it an attributive or adjectival participle, describing or telling us something about Mary. The word "being" [ouse] in the phrase "being pregnant" is also a participle, but it does *not* have a definite article nor is it linked to the preceding participle by the Greek word *kai* ("and"). This means that *ouse* is an adverbial or circumstantial participle. Such participles usually have some adverbial nuance, such as time, cause, concession, means, condition, or the like. The two most likely candidates for the nuance in the phrase "being pregnant" are "because she was pregnant" or "although she was pregnant."

## CHAPTER 5: MARY'S SONG—AND ZECHARIAH'S

1. Tremper Longman III and Daniel Reid, *God Is a Warrior* (Grand Rapids: Zondervan, 1995), 112.

2. See Darrell L. Bock, *Luke 1:1–9:50*, Baker Exegetical Commentary on the New Testament (Grand Rapids: Baker, 1994), 155; see also I. Howard Marshall, *The Gospel of Luke*, The New International Greek Testament Commentary (Grand Rapids: Eerdmans, 1978), 83–84.

## CHAPTER 6: THE *KATALYMA*

1. Walter Bauer and Frederick W. Danker, "katalyma," in *A Greek-English Lexicon of the New Testament and Other Early Christian Literature*, 3rd ed. (Chicago: University of Chicago Press, 2000), 521. Danker writes: "K[atalyma] is therefore best understood

here as *lodging . . .* or *guest-room*, as in [Luke] 22:11; Mk 14:14, where the contexts also permit the sense *dining-room* (cp. 1 Km 1:18; 9:22; Sir 14:24)."

## CHAPTER 7: THE HUMILIATION OF JESUS' BIRTH

1. Craig Keener, "Nativity of the Lord (Christmas Day), Years A, B, C," in *The Lectionary Commentary: Theological Exegesis for Sunday's Texts* (Grand Rapids: Eerdmans, 2001), 3:299.

2. My brother-in-law Rev. Henry Admiraal preached a message on this aspect of the condescension of Jesus at Christmas under the title, "God in Diapers." I thank him for the contrasts developed in this paragraph.

## CHAPTER 8: THE ANGELS ON THE FIELD OF BETHLEHEM

1. Luke Timothy Johnson, *The Gospel of Luke* (Sacra Pagina; Collegeville, MN: Liturgical Press, 1991), 49–50. See also I. Howard Marshall, "host, army," *Gospel of Luke: A Commentary on the Greek Text*, The New International Greek Testament Commentary (Grand Rapids: Eerdmans, 1978), 111.

2. Christopher Evans, *The Gospel of Saint Luke*, Trinity Press International Commentary on the New Testament (Philadelphia: Trinity Press International, 1990), 206.

3. F. L. Godet, *Commentary on Luke* (1887; reprint, Grand Rapids: Kregel, 1981), 91.

4. John Nolland, *Luke*, Word Biblical Commentary (Dallas: Word, 1989), 108.

5. Joel B. Green, *The Gospel of Luke*, The New International Greek Testament Commentary (Grand Rapids: Eerdmans, 1997), 136.

6. Darrell L. Bock, *Luke 1:1–9:50*, Baker Exegetical Commentary on the New Testament (Grand Rapids: Baker, 1994), 219.

7. These passages are all discussed in detail in my "The Heavenly Army on the Fields of Bethlehem," *Calvin Theological Journal* 43 (2008): 301–11.

8. Jeremiah 7:18 has a unique set of circumstances; see the above article for details.

9. Note that Hosea 13:4 reads differently in the Septuagint, the Greek version of the Old Testament: "And I am the Lord your God, who establishes heaven and creates the earth, whose hands created all the army of heaven, and I did not reveal them to you to follow after them; and I led you forth out of Egypt, and you shall not gain knowledge of any god besides me, and there is no Savior besides me." Our English Bibles reflect the Hebrew text.

10. Leland Ryken et al., ed., "Heavenly Armies/Host," in *Dictionary of Biblical Imagery* (Downers Grove, IL: InterVarsity Press, 1998), 372.

## CHAPTER 9: THE SONG OF THE ANGELS

1. For those who know Greek, if *eudokia* is accepted as the correct reading, it is in the nominative case and in apposition to *eirene*, "peace." But if the word is indeed *eudokias*, as the older and better manuscripts read, this is a genitive case, probably a genitive of description (describing who these "men" are).

2. William D. Mounce, *Mounce's Complete Expository Dictionary of Old and New Testament Words* (Grand Rapids: Zondervan, 2006), 502–3.

## CHAPTER 10: THE WORDS OF SIMEON

1. Joseph and Mary's poverty offering is another indication that the presentation in the temple preceded the visit of the magi, when the family received gold as one of the gifts.